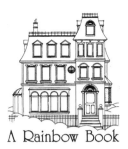

A Rainbow Book

D1357878

# The Successful Retirement Guide

*Hundreds of Suggestions on How to Stay Intellectually, Socially and Physically Engaged for the Best Years of Your Life*

R. KEVIN PRICE

Rainbow Books, Inc.
FLORIDA

## Library of Congress Cataloging-in-Publication Data

Price, R. Kevin, 1947-
  The successful retirement guide : hundreds of suggestions on how to stay intellectually, socially and physically engaged for the best years of your life / R. Kevin Price. — 1st ed.
     p. cm.
  ISBN-13: 978-1-56825-115-8 (trade softcover : alk. paper)
  ISBN-10: 1-56825-115-7 (trade softcover : alk. paper)
  1. Retirement. 2. Retirees—Life skills guides. 3. Retirement—Planning. I. Title.
  HQ1062.P77 2008
  646.7'903—dc22

                         2008019779

*The Successful Retirement Guide: Hundreds of Suggestions on How to Stay Intellectually, Socially and Physically Engaged for the Best Years of Your Life*
© 2009 by R. Kevin Price

www.SuccessfulRetirementGuide.com

ISBN-10: 1-56825-115-7  •  ISBN-13: 978-1-56825-115-8
*Published by*
Rainbow Books, Inc., P. O. Box 430, Highland City, FL 33846-0430

*Editorial Offices and Wholesale/Distributor Orders*
Telephone: (863) 648-4420  •  Email: RBIbooks@aol.com
www.RainbowBooksInc.com

*Individuals' Orders*
Toll-free Telephone (800) 431-1579  www.AllBookStores.com

Disclaimer: The information contained in this publication is not intended to serve as a replacement for professional assistance. Any use of the information in this publication is at the reader's discretion. The author and the publisher specifically disclaim any and all liability arising directly or indirectly from the use or application of any information contained herein. A competent professional should be consulted regarding your specific situation. Further, the author and/or the publisher have not and will not receive any financial consideration for any recommendation of various sources provided that have items such as services and/or goods of any kind for sale. Further still, references are made to a number of Internet sites; at the time of writing, these sites did not contain, to the best of the author's and/or the publisher's knowledge, material that might be offensive to general standards of decency.

The paper used in this publication meets the minimum requirements of the American National Standard for Information Sciences—Permanence of Paper for Printed Library Materials, ANSI Z39.48-1984.

First Edition 2009

14  13  12  11  10  09        7 6 5 4 3 2

Printed in the United States of America.

To all those whose
values, dreams and passions
will help lead to
a new model for retirement.

# Contents

### For the Best of Your Life:  From Acting to Zen

# ■ Acknowledgments ——————————

My thanks go to the many people who were supportive of this project and in particular to the readers of my drafts — Emmett and Marsha Casey, Georgia Feigel, Keith Fowler, Kathleen Flaherty, Jim and Linda Sage, Kathryn Upham.

My wife, Barbara Price, contributed substantially to the content, and, in addition to reading and commenting on multiple drafts, provided the very helpful perspective drawn from her consultancy in gerontology.

Finally, many thanks to Betty Wright at Rainbow Books for her support, coaching and perspective on what works and what doesn't.

*Twenty years from now*
*you will be more disappointed*
*by the things that you didn't do*
*than by the ones you did do.*
*So throw off the bowlines.*
*Sail away from the safe harbor.*
*Catch the trade winds in your sails.*
*Explore. Dream. Discover.*

—Mark Twain

"Successful retirement."

What makes a retirement successful . . . or not?

Financial resources? Health? Friendships? Family? A long life? Time to relax? Time to spend doing things you love? Time to spend trying new things you never had before?

Certainly all of the above factors, as well as others, have a bearing on the quality of retirement. The premise of this book is that the single most important factor in a successful retirement is the extent to which you remain intellectually, socially and physically engaged with life. This introduction explains why this is the case; and the remainder of the book gives you the opportunity to explore ways to make your retirement a successful one.

15

Average life expectancy has increased dramatically in the last century. For people age 65, it now averages an additional 17 years for men and 20 years for women. If you want to check out how long you might live there are several interactive online tools (see Appendix A) you can use. It can be an eye-opening experience. The author, for instance, (a 61-year-old male in reasonable health), is projected to live until 92. That means I have many years during which I may not be in the traditional workforce. Assuming your life expectancy is not dissimilar to mine, what are you and I going to do with all this time?

To maintain mental/cognitive well being we need to exercise our brains in new and challenging ways. Ballroom dancing, solving puzzles, learning a foreign language are all excellent activities. And it is important to note that research proves that you can continue to learn and develop at any age and stage of life. Don't believe that ancient adage: "You can't teach an old dog new tricks," because you can. It may take a little longer, the teaching techniques might need to be modified, but the boom in life-long learning programs and the continuing appeal of Elderhostel all demonstrate the appetite for new and challenging learning opportunities for the mature adult.

A plethora of research demonstrates that to maintain physical well being we need to exercise and live a healthy life. (Have you checked your life expectancy yet?) You can also learn about the physical aging process — what is normal and what isn't. It's surprising how little most of us know about what to expect as we age and what we can do to offset age-related declines.

Remaining socially engaged or meaningfully connected with others is equally important. This can be harder if you are no longer in the workforce and work's built-in social circle is no longer available to you. There are many ways to fill that gap, ranging from joining clubs to spending more time with family, taking classes or volunteering. Many individuals find that retirement is the time for creativity, exploration, continued learning and for giving back. With giving back, you get to share wisdom; you can give advice, mentor, care for and nurture others. What a wonderful opportunity to enhance your life while helping others!

So, how do you begin deciding what you are going to do in retirement? Once you get past the business of cleaning out the closets, organizing the pictures, updating your will, etc. (useful and rewarding tasks certainly), you will probably be ready for more.

The first step is to realize that retirement is an ongoing process of discovery, of trying new things or revisiting those you haven't had time for in years.

The second step is to become informed about the many opportunities and challenges that are waiting for you, hence this book.

As you read through the hundreds of activities that you might do in retirement, please keep an open mind. Think back to childhood when trying a new sport or instrument or game was natural and fun. Keep in mind that there are many different ways to enjoy these activities. You might be interested in taking a class to learn more about a particular activity, while your spouse might be more inclined to join a club and experience it, and someone else would rather read a book about it.

The third step is to try some of the activities. Ideally you'll want to participate in a mix that will challenge you mentally and physically while enabling you to remain socially engaged and productive. This mix will be different for each of us and will change over time. There's no right or wrong way to retire. We are all different, with different experiences, educational achievements, physical capabilities and financial means. The important thing is: You are what you do. Do the best you can with what you've got. You'll be pleasantly surprised at how easily new joy and excitement comes into your life.

Most of the hundreds of activities discussed in this book make reference as to whether they're good candidates, in the author's opinion, for intellectual, social and/or physical engagement. The author's opinion is, of course, only a starting point. As a simple example, if crossword puzzle activities are listed as a possible source of intellectual engagement, you might do them with a friend and add a social dimension, or discuss them while taking a stroll and add a physical dimension.

For most activities there are references. Books, magazines, web sites and other resources can provide additional information about the hundreds of activities listed. These references are, of course, only presented as starting points. Use them as you like.

This book was written to inform, educate and entertain you. I hope you accept the hundreds of opportunities presented in that spirit.

Let me also say that if you believe the author has omitted a valuable activity that should be included in future editions of this book or you have additional knowledge on any subject that might be helpful to future readers, I can be reached at

rkprice@SuccessfulRetirementGuide.com

Here's wishing you a successful retirement!

–R. Kevin Price

# FOR THE BEST
# OF YOUR LIFE

*from*

# Acting

*to*

# Zen

## ACTING

Opportunities:  intellectual, social

All the world's a stage! Literally. And we are all players. Perhaps you have performed on a theatrical stage; perhaps you haven't; but we all, on occasion, have worked to make a personal impression; we have pretended to be or not to be . . . whatever; we have feigned interest or lack thereof; we have imitated; we have impersonated; we have used gestures to back up our vocal communications. In short, while our skill levels may vary, we are all experienced actors. So, since you're so experienced, you might want to consider acting for personal development and satisfaction as well as socialization.

Many communities have amateur theater groups. Many of these offer workshops or classes. You could also check in with your local library or at a nearby college or university for classes. You can also just jump right in. Many amateur performances don't require any particular skills, and folks of all ages, sizes and appearances may be needed.

If you are reluctant to "jump right in," consider some of the ancillary roles needed in amateur theatre: set design and manufacturing, costuming, stage management, lighting, sound, marketing, ticket sales, ushering (get to see the plays for free). You can be part of the production while watching and learning about whether you might like to try for an acting role.

If you do decide to try acting, you may need to audition. An excellent book on the subject is Joanna Merlin's book (listed in Resources on the next page). It provides good advice to actors and anyone else who wants to make an impression (and may have to deal with getting rejected).

Even if you decide not to be an active actor, learning about the art of acting, about actions, objectives, obstacles, relationships, relaxed physical control, listening and reactions can be very rewarding in their own right and assist you in your daily relationships.

## Resources for Getting Started

*An Actor Prepares, and ...*
*Building A Character, and ...*
*Creating A Role*
Constantine Stanislavski, et al.
Theatre Arts Books, Reprint 2002

*Acting Truths and Fictions*
Lawrence Parke
Acting World Books, 1995

*Auditioning – An Actor-Friendly Guide*
Joanna Merlin
Vintage Books, 2001

List of Acting Schools:
www.talentresources.starsearchcasting.com/
acting_schools_camps_actors

www.aact.org (community theater)

# ADOPT-A-HIGHWAY OR ROAD, AVENUE, STREET, LANE

Opportunities:  social, physical

So, I was cruising along a road in California and noticed a sign proclaiming: "This section of highway maintained by Bette Midler." I immediately slowed down in an effort to catch a glimpse of the Divine Miss M at work. Alas, it was not to be; it was not her day for highway work.

According to various national and state studies, the life spans of some items discarded along highways are . . .

> Glass bottles and Styrofoam containers:  1 million years
>
> Disposable diapers:  550 years
>
> Aluminum cans:  200 to 500 years
>
> Plastic six pack cover:  450 years
>
> Tinned cans:  90 years
>
> Rubber boots:  50 to 80 years
>
> Leather shoes:  30 to 40 years
>
> Plastic bags:  10 to 20 years
>
> Cigarette butts:  up to 5 years
>
> Fruit skins:  2 to 5 weeks.

In addition to being ugly, highway litter is a safety hazard. It can kill or injure aquatic, bird and animal life through poisoned water, swallowed butts and sharp edges (glass and metal). Discarded butts can cause fires. Trash can block drains causing flooding, road deterioration and accidents.

Cleaning up litter also reduces litter over time. Studies have shown that people are more likely to litter in areas that are a mess ("Nobody else seems to care, so why should I?") and less likely to litter in areas that are clean.

Want to help? All states, except Vermont, have an adopt-a-highway program. Type "adopt-a-highway" and your state's name into your browser and you should get a hit. Or write to your state's Department of Highways or Transportation for more information.

What if you are in Vermont? Vermont has a "Green Up a Roadside" program that is similar to adopt-a-highway but uses no signs or billboards. Type that name into your browser or contact the Vermont Agency for Transportation for more information.

And before the Longhorns come after me, I should note that the adopt-a-highway program was invented in Texas in 1984. But I would also note that Vermont's Green Up a Roadside program dates from 1970.

## ANIMALS

Opportunities: intellectual, social, physical

Animals provide many opportunities for getting involved in fun and valuable activities. Beyond having animals simply as pets, you might consider, depending on your type/level of interest and real estate/financial wherewithal:

Breeding (possible source of income);
Boarding and/or grooming (for fun or profit);
Humane Society or "rescue" operations;
Observing animals in the wild (local wildlife or go on safari);
Pet therapy (taking your pet to nursing homes or hospitals);
Preserving animal habitat;
Raising animals for their products, such as milk, eggs or wool;
Shows or competitions;
Training dogs to assist the blind;
Volunteering at zoos as a curator or docent.

As we learn about animals and their behaviors, we usually learn about ourselves and our own behavior. As we care for animals, we act out of our most honorable instincts.

## Resources for Getting Started

*Understanding Animal Breeding*
Richard M. Bourdon
Prentice Hall, 1999

*Kennels and Kenneling*
Joel M. McMains
Howell Book House, 2000

www.hsus.org (Humane Society)

www.aazk.org/zoo_career.php

(See also Aquariums, Birds, Cats, Dogs and Pets.)

# ANTHROPOLOGY

Opportunities:  intellectual, social
(if you travel and/or take classes)

Anthropology is the study of humankind. Clearly, this is a huge field of study, and as such it has a number of subsets: anthropogeography, the study of human migrations and geographical distribution; anthropography, the study of the distribution of humans as distinguished by physical character, language, institutions, and customs; cultural anthropology, the study of human culture especially with respect to social structure, language, law, politics, religion and art; ethnology, the study of racial origins and distribution; and physical anthropology, the study of human natural history and evolution.

Anthropological study can provide fresh insights into humankind and all of its multicultural, multiracial, multiethnic diversity. As the world grows ever smaller and we come into closer contact with each other, we can use all the understanding and perspective available to us about who we are and how we got this way, the sources of our differences and the forces that bind us together.

If you are thinking of delving into a new field, why not study your own species? You can begin with one of the above subsets and see where it takes you.

## Resources for Getting Started

*Anthropology*
Carol R. Ember et al.
Prentice Hall, 2001

*Cultural and Social Anthropology*
John Monaghan, et al.
Oxford University Press, 2000

www.aaanet.org (American Anthropological Association)

www.publicanthropology.org (Public Anthropology)

# ANTIQUE COLLECTING ─────────────

Opportunities:  intellectual, social

Generally, anything over 100 years old can be deemed an "antique." (Automobiles are antiques if they date from before 1950.) Your author personally aspires to becoming a non-automotive antique, but if and when the time comes, will decline to be part of a collection.

People have been collecting antiques since they had enough time, money and interest in things from the past to do so. They might begin with something they inherited, something that caught their eye in a shop, something that "fit" into their abode, something that related to career, avocation or spiritual interests, or perhaps just with a fascination with something that is old and functional.

What might attract you to be an antique collector? Here are some traditional antique categories to get your mind going . . .

Books
Bottles
Decorative items: metal, glass, ceramics, posters, metal ware
Glass: drink ware, decanters, paperweights, cut glass
Furniture: chairs, tables, sideboards, chests, etc.
Maps
Marbles
Silver and other metal craft
Stocks and Bonds
Timepieces: clocks, watches
Toys: teddy bears, dolls, toys (wood, tin, die cast, lead)
Tools

Some developing categories . . .
Cameras
Computers
Pens
Radios
Telephones
Typewriters
And many others to which your mind might roam.

## Resources for Getting Started

Auctions (live on eBay)
Antiques stores

Thrift stores

Fairs

Flea markets

Swap meets

Publications

*How to Make a Profit Buying & Selling Antiques &*
*Collectibles Without Really Trying: The Almost Complete*
*Guide to Antique Collecting*
Mark Roeder
iUniverse, 2003

*Treasures in Your Attic*
Joe Rossen, Helaine Fendelman
Collins, 2001

www.antiqueweb.com

www.kovel.com

(*See also* Collecting, *includes items not antique.*)

## ANTIQUE REFINISHING ———————————

Opportunities:  intellectual, physical

Refinishing antiques can add value to a collection (see also above) or can be satisfying in its own right — such as finding out what is under all those layers of paint and varnish, taking something that is tarnished and battered and making it shine again, creating a nice addition to your living space. It can also be a source of income, if you do it for others. (In this case, you will need space, patience, ventilation and elbow grease.)

## Resources for Getting Started

*Refinishing Old Furniture*
George Wagoner
McGraw Hill Professional Publishing, 1990

www.woodfinishsupply.com/articles.html

www.interiordec.about.com/od/furniturerefinish

# AQUARIUMS

Opportunities:  intellectual, social

Did you have a pet goldfish as a kid? Did you press your nose up against the glass of the saltwater tank of marine fish in your dentist's office, while some Yellow-tailed Blue Damsels drifted past? Have you snorkeled over a coral reef and listened to the absolute racket made by fish as you watched them munching on the coral?

If your memories are favorable, perhaps you'd like to explore having an aquarium in your home. Then you can watch fish to your heart's content.

As with any pet decision, it makes good sense to educate yourself before hurrying down to the local pet store to load up on gear and guppies. While introductory books and web sites are listed below for your reference, considerations include:

*Fresh water or salt water?* Fresh water is generally considered to be easier to work with and is the medium with which most aquarium-keepers start.

*Tank size*: Bigger (20 gallon or more) is better. A bigger tank is more stable (temperature and water chemistry-wise), forgiving of errors and gives your fish room to grow. A 20-gallon tank would be about 24x13x16 inches (LxWxH).

*Filtration system*: There are mechanical, biological and chemical systems. You might choose to use a combination of them.

Water will also need to be aerated (aerators send bubbles to the surface helping oxygen to enter the water and undesirable gases to depart) and warmed (aquarium fish generally like water around 73 degrees Fahrenheit to 79 degrees Fahrenheit).

You will also want to light your aquarium and add environmental features such as gravel, rocks and plants to give your fish places to explore and make your tank a more interesting display piece.

## Resources for Getting Started

*The Simple Guide to Freshwater Aquariums*
David E. Boruchowitz
TFH Publications, 2001

*Saltwater Aquariums for Dummies*
Gregory Skomal
For Dummies, 2001

*The New Marine Aquarium: Step-by-Step Setup and Stocking Guide*
Michael S. Paletta
Microcosm Ltd., 2001

www.seaworld.org/infobooks/Aquarium/Aquarium

www.aquahobby.com

www.FishTankGuy.com

## ARCHERY

Opportunities:  social, physical

Can I interest you in some *arco nudo*?

*Arco nudo* means a bare bow, a simple bow (for shooting arrows) with no sights or stabilizers; sort of like Robin Hood's English long bow or perhaps the bow you made from a tree branch and a piece of string as a child.

People still use bare bows, but as in most areas of human endeavor, technology has made an impact. New materials used in conjunction with lamination techniques produced shorter bows with greater power. The addition of pulleys and cams reduced the effort needed to draw the bow (pull the string back to the point at which you are prepared to release it and send your arrow on its intended flight path). Add in counterweights, sights and stabilizer bars and your bow could begin to look quite sophisticated and futuristic — quite an evolution for one of the world's oldest weapons.

While the history of the bow as a weapon goes back at least to the ancient Egyptians, the advent of the gun marked the beginning of the transition of archery to a recreational activity. It is an Olympic sport, and there are local, state, national and international competitions.

You can participate in indoor and outdoor target shooting, field archery (shoot at targets while hiking through the woods), combine target shooting with cross country running or skiing or simply compete to see how far you can shoot an arrow (flight competition). Of course, you need to take care that neither creatures nor property will be injured by your activity.

You don't need to buy fancy equipment to get started, but if you become attracted to the sport there may be "must have" equipment.

Archery can help you build skills, strength, focus, concentration, patience, relaxation and friendships.

The International Archery Federation (officially: The Fédération Internationale de Tir à l'Arc or FITA) is the world governing body (they write the rule books) for archery.

## Resources for Getting Started

*Beginner's Guide to Traditional Archery*
Brian J. Sorrells
Stackpole Books, 2004

*Precision Archery*
Steve Ruis, Claudia Stevenson
Human Kinetics Publishers, 2003

www.archery.org (FITA site)

www.usarchery.org (a list of archery clubs around the country)

# ARCHAEOLOGY ————————————————

Opportunities: intellectual, social

Archaeology focuses on understanding the past by studying its material remains. This can be done from the ease of your reclining chair with book in hand, on the Internet, in the field, in class or any combination thereof.

It is important to note that archaeology is not just the study of things or artifacts, but those things in the context or setting where they are found: caves, fields, battlegrounds, camps, factories, mines, villages, etc. It is the difference between just collecting things and understanding how and when those things were used or manufactured, who used them and why they were left where they were found.

There is opportunity for amateurs (with training and guidance) to do valuable work. This can entail researching abandoned churches, farms, mills, factories, houses, etc. (somebody still owns this stuff; therefore, be sure to get permission before you start poking around), or you may be able to help out in a real dig (many opportunities develop as a result of civil or commercial development projects).

## Resources for Getting Started

*The Amateur Archaeologist's Handbook*
Maurice Robbins
Harper& Row 1981

*Abandoned New England*
William F. Robinson
New York Graphic Society, 1976

*The Archaeological Coursebook: An Introduction to Study Skills, Topics and Methods*
Jim Grant et al
Routledge, 2001

*Adventures in Archaeology*
Anne Ward
Larousse and Co., 1977

www.archaeology.org (excellent magazine and web site)

www.cr.nps.gov/archaeology.htm (lots of information and resources)

www.nps.gov/history/archeology/public/certify.htm
(how to become a certified field archaeologist)

Also consult your local university or state archaeologist's office.

## ARCHITECTURE ———————————————

Opportunities: intellectual

The study of architecture can be very rewarding. It can cover the whole of human history or just the houses in your city or town. It has ties to shelter, religion, politics, engineering, material science, construction techniques, decorative arts, music, theater and many other aspects of human endeavor.

You can focus on the technical aspects (say, understanding the force needed to counter the downward and outward thrust of a rounded arch), the artistic elements or anything in between. You may wish to consider the evolution of architecture as it relates to different cultures, e.g. Western, Islamic, Japanese, Indian, African, Mesoamerican or what exists around you. The remainder of this section describes some ways you might begin your study.

*Historical development:* begins with Egypt and moves onto classical Greece and Rome. Learn about post and lintel construction, column design, development of the arch, tunnel and groin vaults, and domes. Then move onto Gothic and Renaissance architecture. When you meet up with Andrea Palladio (1508–1580) you will have arrived at the beginning of architecture as a profession and can decide to stay in Europe, move to the Middle or Far East or onto the New World.

*Religion*: Many of the great works of architecture have their origins in religion (sometimes several religions). Consider temples, mosques, churches, cathedrals, basilicas or all of the above. Looking at these chronologically would be helpful.

*U.S. housing styles and features*: Americans have drawn their housing styles from all over the world and developed a number of new ones. There are at least 60 distinct styles, e.g. Cape Cod, Federal, Georgian, French Normandy, Greek Revival, Italian Villa, Swiss Chalet, Victorian, Eastlake, Monterey, Mission, Bungalow, Shotgun, Foursquare, and a number of subsets. It can be fun to learn about these and be able to identify the styles in your town or places you visit.

It can also be interesting to learn about the various styles of windows, e.g. Palladian, circle head, fan, oriel; roofs, e.g. hip, gable, gambrel, mansard; and ornamentation, e.g. column types with their entablatures, art deco, gingerbread, tracery and quoins that help create housing style.

*Destination architecture*: So, you're going on a trip to another country, state or town? In addition to a guidebook, why not read a bit about the architecture you are likely to encounter? It could make your trip more enjoyable and educational. For example, you are probably familiar with the triangular gables (front apex of a roof) seen on many American houses, but if you visit the Netherlands or Belgium, you will be treated to gables shaped like bells, 90-degree steps, rounded steps and bottlenecks, with all manner of ornamentation. Before you head off, try picking up a book in your library or simply type your destination and the word "architecture" into your web browser.

*Architecture of your ancestors*: Even if you are not traveling there, studying the architecture of the land(s) of your ancestors can be both fun and educational.

*Period architecture*: If you are interested in a particular time in history, e.g. medieval Ireland, ancient Africa, imperial China, the American Civil War, consider adding an understanding of the architecture of the era to help round out your knowledge.

Your local library will have books on architecture. Pick up a general survey text and test your interest.

## Resources for Getting Started

*The Story of Architecture*
Jonathan Glancy
DK Publishing, 2000

*A World History of Architecture*
Marion Moffett et al.
McGraw-Hill Professional, 2003

*A Visual Dictionary of Architecture*
Francis D. K. Ching
John Wiley, 1996

www.buffaloah.com/a/DCTNRY/vocab.html
(a great web site w/lots of info and photos)

# ART

Opportunities:  intellectual, social

Art is a very large subject. It can include painting, etching, sketching, sculpture, dance, music, architecture, photography, textiles, jewelry and your grandchild's crayon drawing of you mowing the lawn.

The focus here is on providing a general frame of reference for thinking about things to do art-wise. Additional information and suggestions can be found in sections on architecture, dance, music, sculpture, etc.

One approach – and perhaps a good way to get started – is to study art history. While you could begin with the modern day and go backwards, it probably makes the most sense to start at the beginning and review how art history builds on itself. Much of the time it is evolutionary; sometimes it is reactionary; sometimes something totally new happens. All you need to get going is a good art history book. Museum visits are also good as are introductory courses at your local college or university. Most general introductory books and courses will tend to focus on paintings, sculpture and architecture.

The main periods you are likely to review (in the history of Western Art) include, in more or less chronological order . . .

> *Primitive/prehistoric*:  Cave paintings, rock carvings and the like.

> *Egyptian*:  Pyramids, temples, tombs and associated carvings and paintings.

> *Near Eastern*:  Carvings, sculptures, paintings and castings of the ancient Levant.

> *Ancient and classical Greece*:  Ancient temples, statues of the gods and athletes, friezes, painted vessels, etc.; followed by more of the same but with a huge leap forward in grace, delicacy, refinement and execution skills. There was increasing interest in art for its own sake (as opposed to worship or simple functionality).

> *Etruscan and Roman*:  The Etruscans worked in a variety of art forms in northwestern Italy at the same time the Greeks (prior bullet) were doing their thing. The Romans conquered the Etruscans and the Greeks (and just about everyone else) and copied Greek art forms. The Romans took civil and religious construction to new levels, e.g. the Pantheon, Colosseum, Circus Maximus, Baths of Caracalla.

> *Early Christian*:  Paintings in catacombs and basilicas, statues.

*Byzantine*:  Panel paintings, mosaics, manuscript illustrations.

*Medieval*:  Pretty much everything from the fall of Rome to the Renaissance. Much of the art was religion-based:  churches, stained glass, frescos, statues, monasteries, manuscript illumination. Significant progress was made in construction techniques for large cathedrals.

*Renaissance*:  Rebirth of the classical age, beginning in Italy. Emphasis was on the classical forms, accurate portrayal of nature, use of perspective and scale. Increased focus on secular subjects. Giotto di Bondone, Filippo Brunelleschi, Sandro Botticelli, Leonardo da Vinci, Michelangelo Buonarroti, Raphael Santi, Tiziano Vecellio (Titian) all worked in this period. (Do you think there was something in the water?)

*Baroque*:  Added emotion, drama, movement, grandeur, complexity and tension.

*Rococo*:  More carefree, light, playful, free and delicate than Baroque.

*Modern*: This encompasses a variety of forms (many of them rebellions against the strict structures of prior periods) including all of the following, more or less in chronological order, beginning about 1860.

> *Impressionism*:  Artists like Monet, Manet, Renoir and Degas took their painting outdoors (as opposed to in a studio), used lots of light and strong colors.

> *Fauvism*:  Use of color went really wild. Think Matisse and Andre Derain.

> *Art Nouveau*:  Very decorative and foliate style applied to painting, sculpture, architecture, glasswork. Tiffany in the United States; Paris subway entrances; paintings by Klimt.

*Deco*: Evolved from Art Nouveau. More use of outlines and geometric forms.

*Cubism*: The work of art begins to fragment and be portrayed in cubes and other geometric forms. Picasso and Gris.

*Surrealism*: Dreams, fantasies, strange juxtapositions come to the fore. Salvador Dali's drooping watches. Marc Chagall.

*Abstract*: No reference to real life figures except in an allusive fashion (those paintings with lots of color and no easily discernable structure about which most of us have said, "Hey, I could do that!").

*Pop* (for "popular"): Art from everyday life for the common person. Andy Warhol's soup cans.

*Op* (for "optical"): Use of geometric forms to convey a sense of movement (and in the process perhaps make you dizzy or leave you with after-images).

## Resources for Getting Started
(art history)

*The Story of Art*
E. H. Gombrich
Phaidon Press, 1996
(first published in 1950 and still going strong)

*Art History*
Marilyn Stokstad
Prentice Hall, 2004

*How to Read a Painting*
Patrick De Rynck
Harry Abrams, 2004

There is, of course, more art in the world than Western Art. You might consider studying . . .

*African Art*: Africa is a huge continent with great diversity of ethnic groups and cultures, and a longer human history than any other major land mass. While much of the focus in the majority of art history books is on ancient Egyptian, Greek and Islamic works and their influence on subsequent Western art, the artistic output of the African continent is as diverse and deep as its population and well worth exploring. It includes much of the Egyptian and Islamic work, but also masks, pottery, sculpture, basketry and architectural art.

## Resources for Getting Started
(African art)

*Africa: The Art of a Continent*
Tom Phillips
Prestel Publishing, 1999

*The Tribal Arts of Africa*
Jean-Baptiste Bacquart
Thames and Hudson, 2002

www.africanart.org

*Asian art* has it all — calligraphy, painting, printing, carpets, ceramics, batik, sculpture, architecture. While the general focus in the art history books is on India, China and Japan, there are a huge number of subsets, reflecting the diverse cultures and histories of the region.

## Resources for Getting Started
(Asian art)

> *Asian Art*
> John Laplante
> McGraw-Hill, 1992
>
> *Asian Art: India, China, Japan*
> Berenice Geoffroy-Schneiter
> Assouline, 2002
>
> www.asia-art.net
>
> www.asianart.com
>
> www.witcombe.sbc.edu/ARTHLinks3.html

*Islamic Art*: Islamic art, other than early Islamic art, generally does not contain images of people, animals or things. The Koran does not directly ban (to the best of the author's knowledge) portrayal of images, however Muslims believe that God is unique and cannot be portrayed and that portrayal of other creatures (which might result in idol worship) should be avoided.

Judeo-Christian ancient writings contain many stories or narratives religious leaders found useful in teaching religion. If the target population for education couldn't read well, paintings and murals helped tell the story for them (hence all the paintings inside places of worship). The Koran relies more on revelation than narratives and story telling; there was not a strong need for pictorial support for education.

However, the Prophet said, "God is beautiful and loves beauty," so the religious basis for Islamic art is very real and substantive but is generally more focused on the decorative arts using floral and geometric designs. It is art for decoration rather than art for the sake of art.

## Resources for Getting Started
(Islamic art)

> *Islamic Arts*
> Jonathon Bloom, Sheila Blair
> Phaidon Press, 1997

> *Islamic Art and Architecture*
> Robert Hildenbrand
> Thames and Hudson, 1998

Another approach to art can be through the study of different artistic mediums and their various subsets, such as . . .

### Architecture
> *Cultural*, e.g. Northern European, Japanese, Islamic
>
> *Historic periods*, e.g. ancient, medieval, modern
>
> *Religious*, e.g. churches, mosques, synagogues, temples
>
> *Civic and governmental*, e.g. meeting places, theaters, plazas, palaces
>
> *Housing*, e.g. single family
>
> *Materials*, e.g. stone, wood, brick, stucco

### Painting
> *Oil* (paint pigment is mixed with an oil like linseed)
>
> *Watercolor* (water is used to disburse the pigment and a gum

binder)

*Egg tempera* (egg yolk is used to bind the paint pigments)

*Acrylic* (a man-made resin is used to bind the pigment)

On canvas, wood, glass, gourds, fabrics, stone

## Etching

Acid is used to "etch" a drawing onto a metal plate, which is then used for printing. The etched sections of the plate hold the ink. Etching was originally used to decorate armor. Rembrandt made it a high art form for prints. Today it is still used in printmaking, seduction ("Would you care to come up and see my etchings?") and the construction of printed circuit boards.

## Sculpture

*Clay*

*Sand*

*Wood*

*Terracotta* (baked clay)

*Soapstone* (soft stone containing a lot of talc; steatite)

*Metal*

## Photography

*Film*

*Digital*

Or you might focus on a particular subject matter, for example . . .

*Landscapes*: Places, towns, seascapes, wilderness, weather, mountains, rivers, contrast of day and night

*Religious*: Art-decoration of places of worship, religious figures and history

*Portraiture*:  People and pets

*History*:  Major figures, events, achievements

*Still life*:  Inanimate objects such as fruits, veggies, nuts, crockery, utensils, musical instruments, you get the picture.

*Nudes*:  Self-explanatory, I assume.

*Abstraction*:  Focus is on lines, forms and color. There may be some relationship to objects in the "real" world or no relationship at all.

*The human condition*:  Fields of endeavor, daily life, city life, country life, sports, war, education, food, drink, animals, vice, virtue, affluence, poverty, excess, want, industry.

Still another approach could be to concentrate on particular artists, groups of artists or artistic schools, such as . . .

*Rembrandt Harmenszoon van Rijn*:  17th century Dutch painter and etcher.

*French Impressionists*:  A group of painters in France who did the impressionist thing from about 1867 to 1886.

*The Hudson River School*:  The first real American school of artists. Artists like Thomas Cole and Asher Durand painted grand vistas of the Hudson River Valley, the Catskills and the White Mountains, reflecting the beauty of the then new world.

Finally, you might create art yourself through . . .

*Painting*

*Sculpture*

*Sketching*

*Photography*

Your life as an artist can begin with some things as simple as a pencil and a pad of paper, or modeling clay. While there are plenty of books and other instructional materials, it may be particularly useful (and social) to take a class in and come to grips with the fundamentals.

## Resources for Getting Started
(subject matter art)

*How Did You Paint That?*
This is a series of books on how to paint people, flowers, seascapes, etc from International Artist Publishing. Publication dates vary based on subject matter.

*Sculpture, Principles and Practices*
Louis Slobodkin
Dover Press, 1973
(A good introduction to the craft)

*Fast Sketching Techniques*
David Rankin
North Light Books, 2000

*Teach Yourself Photography*
Lee Frost
McGraw Hill, 2004

(See also Architecture.)

# ARTIFICIAL FLOWERS

Opportunities:  intellectual, physical

Artificial flowers can be used for your own decorative purposes, as gifts, as decorations on gifts, at parties, at social club functions, as place cards, etc. While they will never replace the organic variety, they have the advantage of not requiring water, being free of pollen and having a much longer shelf life (periodic dusting may be required).

They can be constructed from a variety of materials — wire, paper, foil, ribbon, silk, fabric, shells, clay, glass or whatever material suits your fancy. Alternately, you might buy artificial flowers and use them to make original arrangements.

## Resources for Getting Started

*Everlasting Flowers*
Patricia Crosher
Dover Publications, 1997

*Faux Fabulous Florals*
Colleen Mullaney
Sixth & Spring Books, 2004

www.save-on-crafts.com

# ARTS/CRAFTS

**Note:** Rather than have an artsy-craftsy section, the author has opted to discuss various arts and crafts throughout the book.

# ASTROLOGY

Opportunities:  intellectual, social

How do those newspaper horoscope writers know so much about you? Well, it could be that people (horoscope readers being people) tend to identify with general and vague personality descriptions. And that people tend to accept general descriptions more frequently when they are told they are individualized, e.g. tied to their astrological sign. Or maybe there is more to it!

People notice patterns: When the sun is at a high angle in the sky, it is summer; at a low angle, it is winter. Watching the sun can provide information about when snow will melt, when is a good time to sow crops, to reap your harvest, to go hunting. Looking at the changing patterns of stars in the night can also mark the progress of the seasons. Ocean tides are linked to the phases of the moon. The lunar cycle is similar in length to the female cycle.

The ancients might have wondered about cause and effect, asking if heavenly bodies actually caused things to happen on earth (and with respect to the seasons and tides, the sun and the moon certainly did and do). But what about other things like health, fertility, friendships, success in negotiations or love?

Astrology has been used to make predictions since ancient times, at least as far back as the city-states of Sumeria (currently Iraq) in 3000 BC. It probably developed hand-in-hand with astronomy.

After several invasions, the Sumerians (after in-breeding with the invaders) became the Babylonians. The Babylonians developed the 360-degree zodiac and divided it into twelve parts of 30 degrees each, with each part named after the major constellation located in that part. They could also trace the movement of the then-visible planets through the constellations and predict eclipses.

Over time there were various other invasions of Sumeria/Babylon and eventually along came the Greeks led by that Great Greek,

Alexander. The Greeks took the astrological/astronomical knowledge of the region and carried it to India (establishing the basis for Eastern Astrology) and then back home, where they gave us the word, horoscope (from the Greek *horoscopos* – "I watch that which is rising.").

The "rising" is that part of the zodiac, now called the "ascendant," which is on the eastern horizon on the date and at the place and time of birth of the person, business, nation, event, idea, etc. for which an astrological prognostication is being sought. Astrology is concerned with the "rising" because, as astrology developed, the arrangement of the heavens at the time of birth became a major starting point for analysis.

Astrologers build "birth charts," taking into account the positions of the signs of the zodiac, the celestial "houses" (another 12 part slicing of the heavens), the planets (which include the sun and the moon), and the apparent angular relationships among them. From the birth chart, and such other factors as they deem appropriate, astrologers are then able to provide an interpretation.

There are no hard and fast rules for interpretation, and different astrologers can come to different conclusions (which, of course, leaves you free to develop your own).

You might consider . . .

> *Learning about your own birth chart and horoscope.*
>
> *Learning about those of people you care for and/or with whom you are in frequent contact.*
>
> *Learning about those of people you don't care for* (maybe there is a reason for the way they are).
>
> *Learning to build birth charts and becoming a prognosticator.*

But is it real?

Certainly light and lack thereof, warm and cold, gravity, magnetism and even sunspots are known to affect our lives. But what about Mars?

Michel Gauquelin and his wife Françoise studied the relationship between planetary positions at birth and human behavior. (Michel and Françoise were both psychologists; he was also a statistician and she a demographer.) Their research over a period of thirty years demonstrated a relationship between certain astrological principles and professions to a high degree of statistical validity. The most noted was the "Mars effect" which found that champion athletes tended to be born with Mars in a critical position. Other relationships were scientists and doctors with Saturn, politicians with the moon, military types with Mars and actors and actresses with Jupiter.

## Resources for Getting Started

*The Case for Astrology*
John Anthony West
Viking Press, New York, 1991

*The Scientific Basis of Astrology*
Dr. Percy Seymour
St Martin's Press, New York, 1992

www.astrology.com

# ASTRONOMY

Opportunities: intellectual, social

Not so long ago, before we decided to light up our night skies with floodlights, sodium arc streetlights, casino neon, theater marquees, auto headlights, billboards, amusement parks, shopping mall glow, etc., all to drive the night out of existence, it was possible to see large numbers of stars and the Milky Way on clear nights.

While viewing the night sky has certainly become somewhat problematic in cities, major suburbs and near centers of commerce and industry, it is still possible near many of these areas to view the major constellations, the moon and the major nearby (relatively speaking) planets – Mercury, Venus, Mars, Jupiter and Saturn – with the naked eye. If you are fortunate enough to live a bit farther away from the light pollution or if you have the opportunity to visit the countryside or the desert or spend some time at sea, many more opportunities open up for you.

You don't need any equipment to begin learning about astronomy. You can get information about the night sky from books in the library, from many local newspapers and from web sites located at the end of this topic. Match up what you see at night with what you have gleaned from the reference materials, and you are a budding astronomer! Besides, wouldn't it be cool while walking the porch with your spouse some evening to be able to point out Venus transiting the constellation Orion?

With nothing more than your lawn chair and an appropriate beverage you can count meteors. During a normal night you might see perhaps seven meteors per hour. However, when a meteor "shower" is expected, you might be able to see as many as 200 per hour. If you are really lucky you may catch sight of a *bolide* – a large meteor that is very bright and might even explode.

If you are willing to spend a bit of money, you might consider investing in binoculars. Binoculars open up whole new vistas. Assuming you have reasonable viewing conditions, you will be able to see craters and mountains on the moon, the Milky Way, star clusters, nebulae, some comets, all the major planets and, on a very dark night, perhaps one of the moons of Jupiter or Saturn.

**Note:** Binoculars are rated by their magnification power (the "7" in 7x50) and the size of their objective lenses (the ones at the large end of the binocs) in millimeters (the "50" in 7x50). In handheld binoculars, more is not necessarily better. If magnifications get higher than 10 you need a very steady set of hands to keep things from jumping around. The 7x50s are considered the night glasses of choice for astronomical viewing with 10x70s being about the upper limit for simple handhelds. If you have access to bigger bucks, image-stabilizing binoculars are available for higher magnifications.

And another good thing about investing in binoculars: you can use them in other ways such as animal watching, at sporting events, horse racing, on your boat, etc.

If you get hooked on astronomy, you may wish to consider buying (or perhaps building, if you are looking for an interesting project) a telescope that will enable you to see even more heavenly bodies and in even more detail. You can then move into astrophotography, join an astronomical society, monitor variable stars, discover comets, etc. And the heavens are yours!

## Resources for Getting Started

*Stargazing: Astronomy without a Telescope*
Patrick Moore
Cambridge University Press, Second Edition, 2000

*Star-hopping for Backyard Astronomers*
Alex MacRobert
Sky Publishing, Belmont MA, 1993

*Binocular Astronomy*
Craig Crossen and Wil Tirion
William-Bell, Richmond, VA 1992

*The Backyard Astronomer's Guide*
Terence Dickinson, Alan Dyer
Firefly Books; Revised Edition, 2002

www.skypub.com

www.adc.gsfc.nasa.gov/adc/adc_amateurs.html

www.astromax.org

# ATHLETICS ———————————————————

Opportunities:  social, physical

Athletics provide many opportunities for engagement. You can organize, participate, teach, coach, umpire, watch or undertake a combination of these.

Schools and leagues need help with planning; organizing schedules, equipment and travel; teaching fundamentals; running drills; keeping stats; coaching; and they can always use some friendly spectators to cheer them on.

If you have expertise in a particular sport like tennis, golf, skiing or ice skating, in which participants need to develop their individual skills, you might enjoy sharing your expertise through teaching at clubs, resorts or other facilities. And you might make some money while doing so.

Participation in athletic events or activities obviously depends on your level of interest, physical condition, level of competition in which you might engage and other factors of which you are the best judge. Some people surf into their 80s; take long canoe trips, e.g.

follow the Connecticut River from upstate Vermont to Long Island Sound; bicycle across the country; hike the Appalachian Trail from Maine to Georgia; participate in Ironman-like events, climb mountains and the like. Some of these activities and others are discussed as separate topics elsewhere in this book.

And, of course, you can still participate competitively in a variety of sports such as tennis, baseball, basketball, hockey, handball, races (on foot, skis or skates) with friends, in clubs, in leagues and even in the (senior) Olympics. So you thought the Olympics were just for younger folks? Read on!

National Senior Games Association: The National Senior Games Association is a not-for-profit organization that is dedicated to promoting healthy lifestyles for active adults 50 years old and over through education, fitness and sport. The NSGA spearheads the senior games movement, sanctioning and coordinating the efforts of senior games organizations across the country. The NSGA also serves as one of the United State Olympic Committee's official arms to the 50 and over population and has a seat on the USOC's board of directors.

At the time this is written, there are games in 48 states (all but North Dakota and Oregon) and the District of Columbia. Many of the states welcome competitors who are residents of other states. Not all states have games every year.

The NSGA also organizes national summer and winter games, providing competition in various age groupings, for such games as . . .

**Summer**
> *Archery*
> *Badminton*
> *Basketball*
> *Bowling*
> *Cycling*

*Golf*

*Horseshoes*

*Racquetball*

*Road racing*

*Shuffleboard*

*Softball*

*Swimming*

*Table tennis*

*Track & Field*

*Triathlon*

*Volleyball*

**Winter**

*Alpine skiing*

*Cross-country skiing*

*Curling*

*Ice hockey*

*Snowshoeing*

*Speed skating*

Of course, all sports – individual or team – need spectators and even better, fans! If you choose to be a fan, bear in mind that your team can't hear you cheer them while stretched out on your couch. Try getting out and supporting your local school or college, little league or maybe your state's senior games.

The main point is this: the fact of retirement doesn't mean your participation in athletics at some level and in some fashion has to end, or can't begin. You do need to exercise good judgment about aligning your aspirations with your capabilities. But remember there are lots of opportunities from which to choose.

## Resources for Getting Started

www.seniorjournal.com/sports

www.nsga.com (senior Olympics/provides links to state games)

www.geezerjock.com (for those over 40)

www.sportsci.org/encyc/agingex (discusses aging and exercise)

(*See also* Appendix B.)

---

# AUCTIONS

Opportunities: intellectual, social

Herodotus of Halicarnassum, the Greek historian generally considered the 'Father of History,' reported in about 550 B.C. on the auctioning of women for marriage. In subsequent centuries auctions were used in the slave trade, to unload the spoils of war, to liquidate estates and in other situations in which people wanted or needed to swap assets for the coin of the realm and a more effective exchange method wasn't available.

The word "auction" showed up in the Oxford English Dictionary in 1565. Sotheby's and Christie's opened for business in 1744 and 1766 respectively.

Today you can buy all manner of stuff at auctions: decorative items, toys for your grandkids, cars, vacations, additions for your collection of whatever, other folks' collections of whatever, houses, artwork, wine, animals, services, you name it. You can also sell all this stuff at auction.

Auctions can be fun. You can get some really good deals. You can also pay too much or get ripped off, if not prudent. It is important to know exactly what you're bidding on, its condition and the auction rules. It is helpful to know where your spouse is (if he or she is attending the auction) so you don't wind up bidding against each other (it's happened). And you don't want to get too excited; you could wind up bidding against yourself (that's also happened).

You can learn things at auctions. I attended a guitar auction at Christie's in New York City in 2004 and learned that if Eric Clapton used a guitar to play "Layla" in a public forum, the fact of his having done so would add at least $250,000 to the value of the guitar. I also learned that if I had an appetite for spending that much money on a guitar (I didn't and don't), I could find myself bidding against a teen-ager accompanied by a doting guardian with a fat checkbook.

The Internet has brought us eBay, sort of a 24/7/365 auction. Initially, the thought of buying something that you can't examine firsthand from a person you have never met and most likely never will meet, may seem somewhat reckless. However, eBay has thought these issues through and come up with a system that minimizes risk. All sellers and buyers are evaluated by the people with whom they do business. You can review these ratings and comments and decide if a particular buyer or seller is someone with whom you wish to conduct a transaction. Most sellers (wishing to protect a good rating or improve one) seem to go to great lengths to describe the item for sale in detail and make very clear any wear and tear or other aspect of it that a buyer receiving it in the mail might find objectionable. You can also pose questions about the item directly to the seller. eBay provides training and practice transactions; it is good to work your way through these and watch a few auctions before jumping into the real thing. eBay has been so successful that it has spawned a number of competitors.

## Resources for Getting Started

*The Complete Guide to Buying and Selling at Auction*
C. Hugh Hildsley
WW Norton & Co. Inc, 1977

*Adventures at Auction*
Leslie Hindman
Clarkson Potter, 2001

*eBay for Dummies*
Roland Woerner, Stephanie Becker, Marsha Collier
IDG Books Worldwide, 1999

www.ebay.com (click on "learn about eBay")

# AUTOMOBILE RESTORATION

Opportunities: intellectual, social, physical

Have you ever thought of restoring a classic car?

What is a classic car anyway? "Classic" might suggest historically memorable, evocative of a particular era or perhaps something that has an enduring impact. It probably also suggests older, although I might argue the Porsche Boxster was a classic the moment it rolled off the assembly line.

For some, classic cars may be true antiques; others may focus more on classic sports cars, touring cars, muscle cars, convertibles, maybe even a truck or a jeep. It is whatever fires up your nostalgia. Mine gets fired up by a '56 Ford, an Austin Healy Sprite, a VW Beetle and the Boxster (all of which I have owned). The station wagons, SUVs and Audi Fox that I have also owned don't ring many nostalgia bells.

Why bother? Maybe because it is a piece of history that needs to be preserved; maybe it is just really pretty; maybe you wanted one when you were younger, but it was beyond your grasp; maybe you want to reconnect with something; maybe you like managing big projects. But if you are interested, there are two ways to go, at opposite ends of the spectrum (and a lot in between).

Buy: if you are rolling in dough and know what you want, buy one already restored or pay someone else to do the restoration.

Do it yourself: if you are handy (or can become so) and have the time and space, this could become a very rewarding project.

In between: this is where most of us would be — doing some ourselves but farming out specific items to professionals. Think: mechanical, electrical, paint, bodywork, upholstery. Don't think that the work is necessarily beyond you — I am not mechanically adept, and I was able to change out a piston in my Austin Healy by following a manual's instructions. You can learn a lot in the process and get to meet a lot of people who have similar interests. You need some tools, but many can be rented. What you need most is time and space.

A couple of good books of a general nature are listed below. They can be helpful in determining whether you have a real interest and as a general guide to managing your project. There are also manuals by make of car that can give you detailed guidance. Once you are done, you might consider joining a touring club of restored autos.

## Resources for Getting Started

*Classic Car Restorer's Handbook*
Jim Richardson
HP Books, 1994

*How to Restore Your Collector Car*
Tom Brownell
MBE Publishing, 1999

# BARTENDING

Opportunities: intellectual, social, perhaps physical
(if you like putting on a show á la bartender Tom Cruise)

Does 5:00 p.m. bring to mind tea or cocktails? If the latter, read on. If the former, kindly refer to the section on "tea."

Bartending sounds like work, and it can be, but it is not here for that reason. It is here for skill building: mixology, service, organization, efficiency; and because it provides the opportunity for social interaction, admittedly brief in many instances. You may also get to attend great parties!

You can learn bartending through a school or through your own reading/experience. If you want to present yourself as a professional (better parties, better pay), it can be helpful to have a school's certification.

By the by, where did cocktail get its name? It appears there are many theories, but no definitive answer. Among the more likely stories:

A New Orleans druggist – Antoine Peychaud – invented a drink called a Sazerac, which used a blend of bitters he developed. He served the drink in a French egg cup called a *coquetier,* which was mispronounced as cocktail. Or . . .

A feather from a cock's tail was frequently used to indicate (by placing it in or on the drink cup or mug) that the drink contained alcohol.

## Resources for Getting Started

*The Official Harvard Student Agencies Bartending Course*
Harvard Students Agencies, Inc.
St. Martin's Griffin, 2000

*Bartending Inside-Out: The Guide to Profession, Profit and Fun*
Lori Marcus
Cadillac Press, 2003

www.webtender.com
www.pbsa.com (schools)
www.abcbartending.com (schools)

# BASKET MAKING

Opportunities: intellectual, physical

Can you use basic hand tools? Can you follow a weaving pattern? Consider basket making. Your product can be useful (breadbaskets, flower baskets, wastebaskets, market baskets, Easter baskets) and decorative for you, while forming the basis for an excellent gift when packaged with flowers or food or simply on its own.

Craft stores can sell you the raw materials from which to make baskets. Or, you may wish to start with a kit. Either way, instructional books can be found at web sites and give you detailed guidance.

## Resources for Getting Started

*Basket Making*
Kay Johnson
B.T. Batsford, 1991

*The Weekend Crafter: Basketry*
B. J. Crawford
Lark, 2003

www.basketpatterns.com
www.basketmakerscatalog.com

## BEACHCOMBING

Opportunities: intellectual, social, physical

Beachcombing can yield many treasures: shells, agates, fishing floats, ocean-worn glass, driftwood and miscellaneous flotsam (potentially from all over the world). These can make nice collectibles for you or items that you could sell to other collectors or shops.

You may also find treasures — coins, watches, jewelry — left behind by other beach goers. For these a comb (rake) or even a metal detector may be helpful. Bear in mind that most folks using metal detectors at beaches spend more on the metal detector than they recover in valuables from the sand, so most of the reward must come simply from the hunt rather than what is found.

It can also be interesting to learn to identify marine organisms that live on the shore or are washed ashore by storm or tide. There are many variations depending on your latitude and longitude, and whether your beach is fresh or salt water. So, in looking for help with creature identification you might try either your library or type "beachcombing" followed by your state's name in your web browser to obtain more information.

You might even progress from beachcombing to beach keeping. All sorts of unattractive stuff also washes up on beaches, and you could remove some of that trash at the same time you collect your treasures. Perhaps you could organize a beach clean up day (to be followed by a party, of course).

## Resources for Getting Started

There are a number of books on beachcombing, but most of them, with the exception of a couple that are written for children, appear to be out of print. So, your best source is probably your local library or the web.

www.seashells.org (info on techniques, shell identification and preservation)

(See also Driftwood and Shells.)

# BED & BREAKFAST ———————————————

Opportunities: intellectual, social, physical

Many folks aspire to owning and managing a B&B as a kind of semi-retirement: keeping busy, meeting new people, freedom of running your own business and income. A B&B can deliver on all those fronts and more. You can be *very* busy; there may be people you wish you *hadn't* met; running a business also presents challenges and responsibilities; there are expenses to be managed as well as income to be gained.

Whether you are a good fit for investing in and managing a B&B should be the subject of some serious soul searching. The "Do you have what it takes?" test in the Craig/Davis book below is a good starting point.

If you decide it is right for you, remember: location, location, location. You'll want to create a market niche that will attract customers and keep them coming back. Even if your inn is old, you want it to be in good shape, so that it is attractive to guests and without a heavy maintenance burden. And you need excellent management.

## Resources for Getting Started

*How to Operate a Bed & Breakfast*
Jan Stankus
Globe Pequot, 2003

*The Complete Idiot's Guide to Running
a Bed and Breakfast*
Susannah Craig, Park Davis
Alpha, 2001

www.spitzerhouse.com/Articles/InnkeepersLetter.html

# BEEKEEPING

Opportunities: intellectual, physical

And the bees we are talking of keeping are Honeybees. They produce honey that you can harvest, eat, sell, turn into gifts. They assist in plant pollination. They can be a fascinating study in organization and marshalling of resources. Like traditional pets, they require your time and attention.

They can also sting you (you need to know how allergic you are) and aggravate neighbors, if your hive swarms (swarming happens when the number of bees in the hive exceed the hive's capacity and a bunch take off in search of a new home).

Here's "hive life" in 140 words: Hives have one queen, a few hundred drones and thousands of workers. The queen's job is to lay eggs (around 2,000 per day for up to five years) and give off a scent that allows everyone to know what home and those who live there smell like. The drones hang around waiting to have sex with the queen. The workers tend to the queen and her egg laying, keep the hive clean, gather and store pollen and nectar, guard the hive and kick out the drones in the fall. When the queen gets old and needs to be replaced, the workers select an egg and grow a new queen in a special cell with special food. When the hive gets crowded, the workers send a new queen off with drones and workers to start a new hive.

A beekeeper gets to observe all this while eating and selling honey too, if you want. And, yes, it is more complicated than what I have described. But it can also be fascinating. Even if you decide beekeeping is not for you, learning about it can still be sweet.

## Resources for Getting Started

*Beekeeping for Dummies*
Howland Blackiston
Dummies, 2002

*Beekeeping: A Practical Guide*
Richard E. Bonney
Storey Publishing, 1993

www.beemaster.com (good introduction/beginner lessons)

www.apis.ifas.ufl.edu/beginner.htm

www.ourworld.compuserve.com/homepages/Beekeeping

## BEER

Opportunities: intellectual, social, physical
(managing calories consumed)

Beer offers a variety of activities, consumption being the first and foremost. Thousands of commercially produced beers flourish around the world. They are brewed with a variety of colors, clarities, bouquets, flavor and alcohol levels (US lager beer tends to be about 5 percent by volume; beers around the world range from 2.5 percent to over 15 percent). They may be light and crisp, dark and dense, sweet or bitter. If you have the opportunity to travel, trying new beers along with new food can be both fun and educational. If traveling doesn't fit into your plan, your local beverage purveyor can probably provide some variations for your palette.

Or you might consider organizing a beer tasting. This could function very much like a wine tasting. You might arrange to taste beers from one country or region; beers of a similar style, e.g. wheat beers, ales, stouts or lagers; beers of differing hoppiness or maltiness. Consider using score sheets to help folks sort out their views.

### Resources for Getting Started
(holding a beer tasting)

> *Michael Jackson's Great Beer Guide*
> Michael Jackson
> DK Publishing, Inc. 2000

> *Beer Companion*
> Stephen Snyder
> Simon & Schuster, 1997

www.sallys-place.com/beverages/beer/beer_tasting.htm

www.merchantduvin.com/pages/2_ale_university/
aleu_beer_tasting.html

Beer brewing can also be rewarding. You can do this (the author has). You can get started/try it out with a kit for less than one hundred dollars. And you are allowed (under federal law) to brew up to 200 gallons a year in a two adult household. (It is, of course, possible that some local jurisdictions may have further restrictions).

## Resources for Getting Started
(for brewing beer)

> *New Brewing Lager Book*
> Gregory Noonan
> Brewers Publications, 2003
>
> *Designing Great Beers*
> Ray Daniels
> Brewers Publications, 2000
>
> www.brewery.org
>
> www.homebrewery.com

You might choose to collect beer bottles, cans, mugs, steins, glasses, coasters, pails, advertisements — whatever. Bear in mind that if you collect items still containing brew, the contents will deteriorate over time.

## Resources for Getting Started
(miscellaneous beer)

*Classic Bottled Beers of the World*
Roger Protz
Trafalger Square Publishing, 1997


www.allaboutbeer.com/collect


# BICYCLING

Opportunities: social, physical

You never forget how to ride a bike. On your next trip to the library (assuming a reasonable distance) why not leave your six foot tall, 14 miles to the gallon, six seat SUV in its garage and ride a bike (yours, if you have one, or borrowed, if need be)? You'll get pleasant exercise, see things you won't notice while driving, avoid adding to pollution and save on gas.

A bike equipped with a rack and bungee cords or a set of panniers (the bags that hang on the sides of your wheels) can easily handle short trips to the market, picnics, trips to sporting events and the like. Parking is also cheaper. (Yes, on rainy days the SUV may be a better alternative.)

When riding a bike in most states you are just another vehicle on the road – you follow the same rules that would apply to other vehicles that may be moving in the same direction but perhaps slower than the automotive traffic.

If you wish, bicycles can take you places that cars cannot go (either because they are prohibited or don't fit) like parks and forests. You may also find that may be a good fit for your exercise routine.

If you really get hooked, you might try longer-term (overnight) bike trips, bike clubs or racing. Friends of the author's took three months out of their lives to bike across the U.S. from west to east (or maybe they put three months *into* their lives).

Today's bicycles are available with shock absorbers, comfortable seats and a choice of frames and tires to support the type of riding you will do. A quality bike shop can give you good guidance.

## Resources for Getting Started

*New Cyclist Handbook*
Ben Hewitt, ED
Rodale Books, 2000

www.bicyclinglife.com

www.bikexprt.com/streetsmarts

www.bikewalk.org

# BILLIARDS

Opportunities: intellectual, social, physical (eye-hand coordination)

"Billiards" is a generic name for a large number of games played on a table with balls and a cue. While movies such as "The Hustler" or songs like "Maggie Mae" might lead one to believe it is possible to make a living from this activity, that belief is misguided for most. Billiards is referenced here primarily for its entertainment and socialization values.

Pocket billiards or "pool" is typified by the game most familiar to Americans: *Eight Ball*, in which you try to "pocket" all of the striped balls (numbered 9–15) or solid balls (numbered 1–7) and then the eight ball to win. Other mainstays of pocket billiards are *Straight Pool*, in which you accumulate points by making called shots until you reach a targeted number. *Lineup Straight Pool* is similar to straight pool, except balls are returned to the table when a player ends his turn or when all fifteen balls have been pocketed. *Rotation* is where players score points by hitting the lowest numbered ball on the table and receiving the number value of any balls that are pocketed. *Nine Ball* is similar to rotation except that only the nine lowest numbered balls are used, and the winner is the person who pockets the nine ball.

"Billiards" is also the name of a particular game, not as popular in the United States as "pool," but quite popular in the rest of the world. A Billiard table has no pockets. The game is played with three balls: two white balls (one of which is marked with a dot and called "the black ball") and one red ball. The object of Billiards is to be the first player to achieve a targeted number of points, e.g. twenty. Points are scored by hitting, in any order, three cushions and one of the object balls (either the red or the white) and then hitting the second object ball. Billiard shots can be quite complicated, lengthy and dramatic in comparison to the typical pool shot.

A third major variant is Snooker, prominent in the United Kingdom and countries that comprise the former British Commonwealth. Snooker is played with twenty-one red balls, six colored balls and one cue ball. Points are scored by "potting" (hitting into a pocket) the red and colored balls in the prescribed order.

Billiards can be played in commercial venues established for that purpose, clubs, pubs or in your own home, if you have the space and decide a table would be a worthwhile investment.

**Note:** if you enjoy ping-pong, there are ping-pong surfaces that are designed to fit on top of billiard tables.

It can be good to invest in a rulebook — everyone seems to know the rules but not everyone who "knows" agrees what they are. It is also good to have a discussion about rules before commencing play, so that misunderstandings are avoided. A good guidebook (Robert Byrne's book) can also be helpful in improving your game.

## Resources for Getting Started

*Byrne's New Standard Book of Pool and Billiards*
Robert Byrne
Harcourt Brace & Co., 1998

*The Illustrated Principles of Pool and Billiards*
David G. Alciatore
Sterling Publishing, 2004

www.engr.colostate.edu/~dga/pool
(instructions and video tips)

www3.sympatico.ca/eric.perreault/defaulthtml.html
(billiards guidance)

www.worldsnooker.com

# BIOGRAPHY ―――――――――――――――――――

(See Personal History.)

# BIRDS / BIRDING ―――――――――――――――――

Opportunities: intellectual, social, physical (if out and about)

Do you ever wonder where birds seen only seasonally go in the other seasons? Do you wonder why they go there? Why some birds are content to live in an area year-round? Why some just seem to pass through? Where and how they build their nests? How many broods they have a season? How long they live? What they eat? Is feeding birds a good thing or a bad thing? What kind of nest box attracts what types of birds? How many species of birds live in your area? What is the name of that black bird with the yellow patch on its wings? And just why is it that birds of a feather flock together?

If any of these questions resonate for you, perhaps you would be interested in birding. Birding can range from simply watching for enjoyment to data collection and detailed scientific study.

At its simplest and easiest, you can start birding by just looking out the window. If you wish to attract birds to watch, you might add a bird feeder or two, perhaps a birdbath or some nesting boxes. If your interest grows further, you might even wander outdoors and go for a walk to broaden your birding horizons.

With the addition of a field guide (a guide to birds commonly found in your area) and probably a pair of binoculars, you can begin to identify birds in a more structured fashion by their size, color, shape, markings, behaviors, habitat and song. You might even begin to keep a diary of those you see.

Perhaps you'd like to do your birding activities with others. You can often find bird clubs through bird food stores, park systems, state Audubon Societies and local schools and museums. While birding with others brings companionship, it also offers the opportunity for you to learn from others and share what you have learned with them. You may also be able to get involved with national or regional bird censusing.

If you get really hooked, you can take your birding activity with you to other parts of the country or the world. North America has about 750 species of birds, but there are more than 9,000 additional species elsewhere in the world.

## Resources for Getting Started

*Pete Dunne on Bird Watching*
Pete Dunne
Houghton Mifflin, 2003

*The Audubon Backyard Birdwatcher*
Robert Burton, Stephen Kress
Thunder Bay Press, 1999

www.birdsource.org

www.audubon.org

www.pbs.org/birdwatch

www.mbr-pwrc.usgs.gov/id/framlst/framlst.html

# BIRD HOUSES AND FEEDERS ━━━━━

Opportunities: intellectual, physical

You might want to add bird nesting houses or feeders to your property. You might even want to consider constructing your own houses or feeders. There are at least two challenges here: designing and building a house that birds will want to nest in and keeping squirrels out of the feeder. Both can be fun.

## Resources for Getting Started

*The Big Book of Bird Houses and Bird Feeders*
Thom Boswell et al.
Sterling, 2004

www.npwrc.usgs.gov/resource/birds/birdhous/index.htm

www.mdc.mo.gov/nathis/woodwork/ww1/

## BLOGGING

Opportunities: intellectual, social

A "blog" is short for "we*blog*." It is a website that can be a family gathering place, a public diary, a bully pulpit, a political column, your own news channel (with you as anchor), an advice column, a discussion forum on a topic of your choice, a travel journal or anything you might want to make it. It is easy to set up and run a blog, and it can be free. Web site services, such as those listed in Resources, will assist you in setting up your blog. And it can be done in less than five minutes. Other services like the popular www.typepad.com charge a small fee for their service, but you get more tools for design and blog management.

Why would you want to do this? I have no idea; but *you* may. If you need or have always wanted a forum to make a point, let off steam, share your view of the world or some part of it, connect with others, debate, discuss, accuse, defend, share, whatever, a blog can be your forum.

Setting up a blog can be as easy as:

1.  Visiting one of the blogging services;
2.  Completing some necessary information forms (you can remain anonymous);
3.  Designing your blog page (the service will have tools to help you do this); and
4.  Posting your first thoughts.

It can be helpful for your blog to have a theme of some sort, e.g.

sports, your dog, global warming, hair loss, Moroccan cooking, federal separation of powers. There are millions of blogs and almost as many blogging topics as there are bloggers. Your subject matter can help attract other folks to your blog to read your thoughts and perhaps to comment.

It can also be helpful, if you are comfortable doing so, to include some information about yourself on your blog. People are more likely to comment if they have some idea of the person they're addressing. (But be careful what you share — once it is out there in webland, it is most likely there forever.)

## Resources for Getting Started

*Blogging*
Biz Stone
New Rider Press, 2002

*Blogging in a Snap*
Julie Meloni
Sams, 2005

www.blogger.com

www.wordpress.com

www.livejournal.com

# BLOOD BANK

Opportunities: social

Perhaps you can't single-handedly save the world, but you can save a life.

About every two seconds in the United States, someone needs blood or blood products due to premature birth, injury, disease or surgery. That's over 38,000 pints a day. There is nowhere to get blood except from donations.

If you weigh at least 100 pounds and are in good health, you can save a life. There is no upper age limit for donations. While over 60 percent of Americans are eligible to give blood, only about 5 percent do so. Your body has about 10 pints of blood in it; a normal donation is one pint. Your body replaces the donated blood quickly.

The process is easy: fill out a medical questionnaire; have your temperature, blood iron levels, blood pressure and pulse checked; lie down for about 10 minutes during the donation process; have a bite to eat; and you're a hero.

Your local Red Cross chapter can give you more information about the donation process, and when and where you can donate.

You can also volunteer to help in blood drives. Trained medical professionals manage the actual donations, but help is needed in publicizing the drives and with assisting donors before and after the donation process.

## Resources for Getting Started

www.bloodsaves.com

www.redcross.org

www.givelife.org
(assistance on scheduling a donation appointment)

# BOATING

Opportunities: intellectual, physical, social

People go boating for a variety of reasons: travel, sight-seeing, fishing, adventure, access to places to which there are no roads, entertaining, water-skiing. Many sailing terms have entered our everyday language:

above board, by the board, onboard, overboard;

clean slate, close quarters, cut and run, cut of one's jib;

even keel;

fagged out, fathom;

jack knife;

laid up, landmark, leeway;

over a barrel;

pooped;

skyscraper, spic and span;

taken aback . . . and more.

When boating, there are basically four ways to go: muscle, wind, electric motor or combustion engine. As with most things, costs increase with size and sophistication.

With muscle power, you can power rafts, canoes, kayaks, rowboats and the like and enjoy rivers, lakes, bays, harbors. While some folks will ride rapids or follow rivers for miles, most will not be going too far, and the water will generally be calm.

Sail power can propel you on small bodies of water or across oceans. Simple daysailers can enhance your enjoyment of protected waters. A 40-footer can take you to another continent. With a reasonably well-designed boat and sail, you can sail into the wind, using the same principles that enable airplanes to fly.

Electric power is generally used for motors in small boat fishing and in large nuclear-powered military vessels. Combustion engines are used in everything from the smallest outboards to the largest yachts and commercial vessels.

If you want to enjoy boating, you need to know how to do so safely and responsibly. At a minimum, you need to understand some basic seamanship (docking/undocking, anchoring, navigation, a few knots, use of sails and/or your engine), safety rules and regulations including the "Rules of the Road," how to read weather changes, what to do if someone falls overboard. Lack of understanding can be dangerous for you, your crew, your boat and others. Ignorance can also be financially costly in terms of damage and or fines, e.g. if you pass within 100 yards of a U.S. Navy vessel without permission you could be fined up to $250,000 and/or receive up to a six year prison sentence. And from the author's personal experience, stay even farther away from nuclear submarines underway – they leave a *very* large hole in the water.

Many states offer safe boating programs as do the United States Power Squadrons®, the U.S. Coast Guard Auxiliary, U.S. Sailing and others. There are also commercial courses that can take you from the basics to preparing you for overnight and offshore voyaging.

## Resources for Getting Started

*Chapman Piloting & Seamanship*
Elbert Maloney
Hearst, 2003

*Boater101*
Marine University
Rainbow Books, Inc., 2007

www.uscgboating.org
(U.S. Coast Guard site – lots of info and links)

www.usps.org
(United States Power Squadrons®)

www.sailingcourse.com
(U.S. Sailing)

www.boatus.com/foundation
(BoatU.S. safety and environmental programs)

www.commanderbob.com
(lots of good information and links)

# BOOK BINDING AND REPAIR

Opportunities: intellectual

Have you ever thought about being a bibliopegist? You might have, if you are a bibliophile or a bibliopole or if you have a bibliotheca.

Bookbinders (bibliopegists) have been in business since the ancient Assyrians used clay tablets for writing. However, clay tablets were a bit bulky for books of any length and heavy to check out of the Assyrian library, so the next step up was the scroll using papyrus (plant material) or vellum (originally animal skin, now paper). The Latin word for scroll is *volumen* from which we get our modern word for book – *volume*.

Scrolls could be quite lengthy; they were divided into sections divided by vertical lines. But there was still a lot of rolling and unrolling to get to the section of the scroll you wanted. Eventually someone figured out that the scroll could be cut into pieces, the pieces stacked up and sewn together, and the first book was bound.

Today, with Print-on-Demand capabilities, it is a lot easier to assemble a book from your MS Word file. But what if you wanted to bind together a number of poems or essays you've written, letters you've sent or received, news clippings that are important to you, your children's or grandchildren's drawings and the like? Or what if you have books that are damaged in some fashion – broken spine, torn cover, loose pages, mold/mildew – that are important to you and that you would like repaired?

You could take your materials or books to your local bibliopegist, or you could undertake the task yourself using some of the resources listed here. If you enjoy the work you might also enjoy volunteering your assistance at your local library where books are frequently in need of repair.

## Resources for Getting Started

*Book Repair*
Kenneth Lavender
Neal-Schuman, 2001

*The Book Lover's Repair Kit*
Estelle Ellis
Knopf, 2000
(book on repair plus materials to make the repairs)

*Hand Bookbinding*
Aldren Watson
Dover, 1996

www.cs.uiowa.edu/~jones/book/

# BOOK CLUB

Opportunities: intellectual, social

Book clubs or reading groups can be wonderful ways to stimulate your intellect and social life. You could join an existing group or, in collaboration with others, form one of your own. Whether joining or forming there are a few items you should consider, among them:

Size of the group;

Frequency of meetings;

Location of the meetings;

Theme to the books read, e.g. fiction, history, social issues;

How books are chosen;

Who leads the discussion;

Should the discussions just be on the book or on other adjoining subjects.

## Resources for Getting Started

*Good Books Lately*
Ellen More, Kira Stevens
St Martin's Griffin, 2004

*The Reading Group Handbook*
Rachael Jacobsohn
Hyperion, 1998

www.book-clubs-resource.com
(in-depth advice on starting a reading group)

www.readerscircle.org

(learning about book clubs in your zip code area)

www.readinggroupchoices.com

(in-depth advice on starting a reading group)

## —— BOOKS FOR THE BLIND OR DYSLEXIC

Opportunities: intellectual, perhaps social

If you enjoy reading, perhaps you'd be willing to read aloud and be recorded, so that others who do not have access to the print media can enjoy the same subject matter. If you have a background in math, accounting or in technical or scientific areas, readers are also needed for materials for which the reader's expertise will assist the listener's comprehension.

### Resources for Getting Started

www.rfbd.org

## BRAIDED RUG MAKING

Opportunities: physical

Braided rugs of the homemade variety are generally made from used clothing or material remnants, usually wool, sometimes cotton. Think of the oval or round braided rug you may have seen in your grandparent's parlor.

Braided rugs are sometimes called "rag rugs," because they were literally made from rags during some of our country's more challenging economic times. But they have also been made commercially from new materials. Most home rug braiders use materials they may gather from a variety of sources with one of the most useful being rummage sales.

Basically, the rug is made by taking three strips of material two or three inches across and braiding them together. What you braid is then formed into the desired shape and the braid edges are sewn together to retain the shape. Couldn't be easier! While you can use more sophisticated braids and construction techniques, at its core it is really quite simple.

## Resources for Getting Started

*The Illustrated Guide to Rug Braiding*
Vera Cox
Cox Enterprises, 1995

www.craftown.com/instruction/rugs.htm

www.netw.com/~rafter4/braids.htm

www.motherearthnews.com/library/
1971_November_December/The_Braided_Rug_Go_Round

(See also Hooked Rugs.)

# BRAIN EXERCISE AND TRAINING —————

Opportunities: intellectual, physical, social

"Use it or lose it" applies to our minds as well as our bodies. Studies have shown that our mental skills can be kept in shape through activities that keep our minds active and challenge us to think in new ways. Learning a new language or music theory or how to play a musical instrument have all been shown to be very helpful.

Try doing things with your left hand that you would normally do with your right (if you are right-handed) and vice versa. (Brushing your teeth is an interesting place to start; shaving is not).

Solving puzzles such as crossword, jigsaw, sudoku; playing board and card games, especially if you vary the games you play and take the time to learn new ones; participating in athletic activities, dancing, reading, improving your computer skills, socializing, can all be helpful.

## Resources for Getting Started

*The Memory Workbook*
Douglas Mason et al.
New Harbinger Publication, 2001

*Keep Your Brain Alive*
Lawrence Katz, Manning Rubin
Workman, 1998

www.swedish.org/16194.cfm
(discusses and presents exercises for the brain)

www.helpguide.org/life/improving_memory.htm

# BRIDGE

Opportunities: intellectual, social

The card game of contract bridge has many forebears with the most recent being Harold S. Vanderbilt who assembled the current game in 1925 while waiting to pass through the Panama Canal.

It is a very popular game for four people; it involves an element of luck (the cards drawn), teamwork (working with your partner) and card playing skill. It is also a pleasant way to bring a group of people together for socializing in addition to the card playing.

While it is more substantive than many simpler card games, it is not difficult to learn, and your teamwork and playing skills will increase the more you play. (If you are hesitant to undertake a new learning experience, please (re) read the previous section of this book.) You can also participate in classes and join or perhaps start a group with people of similar playing experience.

The game is called *contract* bridge because play involves trying to reach the number of *tricks* you and you partner have committed to making (the *contract)* if you have been successful during the *bidding process*. A *trick* is one round of play involving a card from each player (there are 13 tricks in a 52 card deck). The *bidding process* is one by which partners try to ferret out how many tricks they can win based on the cards dealt to them (but without showing each other their holdings). The highest bid wins and has the contract. The team without the contract tries, through shrewd card play, to prevent the contract from being achieved. Based on the outcome, points are awarded and another game ensues.

You will hear the terms *rubber* bridge and *duplicate* bridge. A *rubber* is winning two games out of three in social contract bridge. *Duplicate* bridge is used more in tournaments and involves all tables of players being dealt the same hand (luck of the draw is removed).

## Resources for Getting Started

*How to Play a Bridge Hand*
William S. Root
Three Rivers Press, 1994

*The Complete Idiot's Guide to Bridge*
H. Anthony Medley, Michael Lawrence
Alpha, 2004

www.acbl.org
(lessons, software, rules, scoring information)

www.pagat.com/boston/bridge.html

# BRIDGES

Opportunities: intellectual

Bridges, large or small, wood, metal, stone or concrete, we have all traveled over them. We need them to get to school or work or to Grandma's house. They are important for delivery of all the goods and materials we have come to need to support our daily lives.

What kind of bridges are there? How does a bridge "work" (stay in place and carry its load)? What is the lifespan of a bridge? How do they need to be cared for? What kinds of bridges do you have in your area? What is the history of their construction? If you are an engineer, you may have the answers to most of these questions. If you are not, it might be worth exploring bridges.

## Resources for Getting Started

*Bridges of the World*
Charles Whitney
Dover, 2003

*Bridges: A History of the World's Most Famous and Important Spans*
Judith Dupre
Black Dog and Leventhal, 1997

www.howstuffworks.com/bridge.htm
www.pghbridges.com/basics.htm

# BUTTERFLIES

Opportunities: intellectual

There are about 28,000 species of butterflies. Along with moths, they belong to the order *Lepidoptera*, a word derived from the Greek for scales on wings. In the insect world, only butterflies and moths have these scaled wings. Butterflies can range in size from about 0.6 inches to over a foot across.

How do you know whether you are looking at a butterfly or a moth? Butterflies fly during the day and have knobbed antennae; moths fly at night and do not have knobbed antennae.

It can be interesting to learn about butterflies and their lifecycle, and to learn to identify ones that live in your area. You can also grow a garden — summer phlox and asters are particularly effective — designed to attract butterflies.

One of the world's most interesting butterflies is the North American Monarch. Monarchs that emerge from their pupa in the late summer and early fall flit their way to Mexico to spend the winter. They may travel as much as 2,000 miles to get there! In the spring, they migrate back north to lay eggs and begin the process again. (Monarchs born early in the year are breeders only — they don't make the trip south.) The University of Kansas Entomology Department manages a Monarch Watch Program in which you can participate by tagging monarchs, so that their migration patterns can be tracked.

## Resources for Getting Started

*Butterflies of North America*
Jim Brock, Ken Kaufman
Houghton Mifflin, 2003

www.monarchwatch.org (University of Kansas Monarch Watch Program)

www.npwrc.usgs.gov/resource/distr/lepid/bflyusa/bflyusa.htm

www.butterflies-moths.com

# CALLIGRAPHY

Opportunities: intellectual, social, physical

"Calligraphy" derives from two Greek words, *kallos* and *graphos*, which come together to mean "beautiful writing."

Why would you want to learn calligraphy? It is beautiful, and it is useful. While beauty is in the eye of the beholder, let's assume the Greeks had it right. To what uses can it be put? Here are a few of them:

Letter writing;

Greeting cards — birthday, holiday, get-well, retirement;

Invitations;

Poems (for that special someone perhaps);

Business cards;

Announcements;

Certificates;

Menus;

Posters;

Scripture (fantasize yourself as an Irish monk working on the Book of Kells);

Place cards;

Awards;

Flyers;

Name tags;

Your favorite quote;

Someone else's favorite quote (to be given as a gift).

You can do this for fun. You can do this for money. (Check out how much folks get paid to do wedding invitations.)

You don't need artistic talent to be a competent calligrapher; you simply need the time, patience and guidance to develop the skill, and the tools to apply it. If you have the time and patience, your library or the books and web sites listed here can provide the guidance to help get you started. Beginner's tools – pens, ink, straight edges – should cost less than twenty dollars.

## Resources for Getting Started

*Calligraphy*
Don Marsh
North Light Books, 1996

*The Complete Calligraphy Set: Techniques, Tools, and Projects for Mastering Calligraphy*
Ann Bowen
Readers Digest, 2001

www.alphabytes.com/pages/resources/calliglinks

www.42explore.com/calligrphy.htm

www.studioarts.net/calligraphy

www.courses.dce.harvard.edu/~humae105/fall97/twest

# CAMPING

Opportunities: physical, social

Yes, you can still hike into the forest and do the pup tent thing — sit around the campfire (or your burner stove, if open fires aren't allowed) and later listen to the strange noises in the woods while trying to find a comfortable position in your sleeping bag.

But perhaps a campground and an RV, a pop up trailer or a cabin might be more to your liking. Campgrounds have various amenities and are frequently located near hiking, fishing, swimming, boating or scenic attractions. This can be one of the best ways to enjoy our national parks.

## Resources for Getting Started

*Camping Made Easy*
Michael Rutter
Globe Pequot, 2001
(good tent camping guide)

www.nps.gov
(National Park Service site)

www.gocampingamerica.com

www.camping-usa.com

# CANDLE MAKING ─────────────

Opportunities: intellectual

Want to light up your life? Light up someone else's life? Make candles!

Making a basic candle isn't much more challenging than baking muffins: melt the wax, pour it into a mold, cool. There are many mold shapes available; you can even make your own. You can add color, scent and (nonflammable) decorative items.

You can use your candles yourself or make them as gifts that will remind the recipient of you whenever they are used.

You do need to exercise care while melting the wax. Use a double boiler and thermometer. Never leave the melting wax unattended. Have a fire extinguisher nearby.

## Resources for Getting Started

*The Candlemaker's Companion*
Betty Oppenheimer
Storey Press, 2001

*The Encyclopedia of Candlemaking Techniques*
Sandie Lea, Sue Heaser
Running Press, 1999

www.candletech.com

www.wicks-wax-scents.com

www.lonestarcandlesupply.com

# CANDY MAKING

Opportunities: intellectual, social

Sugar, corn syrup, chocolate, nuts, cream, butter — what's not to like?

If you can do basic cooking, you can make candy. Most of what you will need equipment-wise can be found in reasonably equipped kitchens. You may need to add a candy thermometer.

For starters, there are easy recipes for chocolate truffles, popcorn balls (you might have made those as a kid), taffy, fudge, pralines, crunches and barks. You might then move on and add coconut snowballs, dipped pretzels, decorated bonbons, peanut butter chocolate balls, and concoctions using caramel and butterscotch.

For gifts, entertaining, the holidays, Valentine's Day or your own consumption, candy making can be really sweet.

## Resources for Getting Started

*Candy Making*
Ruth Kendrick
HP Trade, 1987

*Truffles, Candies and Confections*
Carole Bloom
Ten Speed Press, 2005

www.countrykitchensa.com/whatshot/
easy_candy_recipes.aspx

www.candylandcrafts.com (recipes and supplies)

# CATS

Opportunities: social

Cat domestication probably occurred about 5,000 years ago with the African wildcat in what is now the Sudan and what was then Upper Egypt. Humans had learned to domesticate and store crops. Stored crops attracted vermin. Cats ate the vermin. Humans appreciated the cats' activity and treated them nicely. A symbiotic relationship formed and continues to this day.

There are almost 80 million domestic cats in the United States. There are more cats than dogs (of which there are about 65 million). More households have dogs than cats, but multiple cat households occur more frequently than multiple dog households.

Compared to dogs, there are several advantages to cats as pets: they are generally smaller; they purr; they can be trained to use a litter box; they can amuse themselves; they may, with appropriate food and water, be left alone for several days; and true to their heritage, they continue to eliminate vermin.

Some disadvantages include: whereas dogs sleep through the night, cats take "cat naps" and are more likely to be on the prowl in the dark; dogs can be trained to follow your oral instructions while cats will do as they damn well please; not being pack animals, cats cannot be herded.

You will also need to determine if your cat will be an indoor-outdoor cat, or strictly an indoor cat. If an indoor-outdoor cat, you will need to contend with an increased possibility of disease, disposal of hunting trophies and treatment of battle scars.

As with all pets, it pays to do research about what is needed to be a responsible pet owner and to ask yourself candidly if you are prepared to accept those responsibilities.

## Resources for Getting Started

*Complete Cat Care*
Alan Edwards
Southwater Publishing, 2001

*Guide to a Healthy Cat*
Elaine Wexler-Mitchell
Howell Book House, 2003

www.catsinternational.org

www.cfainc.org

www.cats.about.com

# CELEBRATE RITUALS, HOLIDAYS, TRADITIONS

Opportunities: social

Do you/did you find while working that you sometimes didn't make the time to celebrate people's birthdays, anniversaries, graduations, retirements or other accomplishments or transitions? (The author did.) "Celebration" doesn't mean party time; it means simply taking the time to call or send a note or card to acknowledge the celebrated event. It always feels good to receive the recognition.

You might consider making a list of those events that recur annually and reviewing it monthly to help you remember to add some good cheer to someone else's life. And when a non-recurring event worthy of celebration occurs, seize the opportunity to send congratulations.

## Resources for Getting Started

Go to a local greeting card shop or your drugstore greeting card section, and there before your eyes are all kinds of suggestions for special days, holidays, traditions and rituals.

# CERAMICS

(See Pottery.)

# CHEESE MAKING

Opportunities: intellectual

We all remember Little Miss Muffet who, while sitting on a tuffet, munched on curds and whey. Did you ever wonder what a "tuffet" is? And how about that "curds and whey" stuff? Well, a "tuffet" is a low seat, and curds and whey are products of the cheese making process.

You can make your own curds and whey, if you'd like to try them, but it might be more fun to go a bit further and make your own cheese. Wouldn't it be fun when someone compliments you on your cheese plate to be able to say: "Thanks! I made it this past weekend."

It is interesting to try and imagine how cheese making was discovered — the key ingredients are milk and enzymes extracted from the fourth stomach of a calf. (Yes, calves have four stomachs.) However it was discovered, cheese making goes back at least as far as the ancient Greeks. Homer tells us how Odysseus and his men entered the home of Polyphemous the Cyclops and ate his cheese while he was out tending his sheep. Polyphemous, quite miffed, responded by eating some of Odysseus' men. Odysseus gave Polyphemous a sharp stick in the eye. This angered Polyphemous' dad – Poseidon – who condemned Odysseus and his men to a long sea voyage. But back to cheese . . .

You can make cheese in your own kitchen. And you don't need the fourth stomach of a calf to do it. For simple cheese production, you'll need milk, a curdling agent – either something acidic (like lemon juice) or an enzyme, a thermometer, stainless steel or glass pots and measuring cups, stainless steel spoons and cheesecloth. If you wish to progress into more sophisticated cheeses, you might want to invest in molds (for shaping) and a press.

Essentially cheese is made by curdling milk. The curds produce the cheese – soft or hard, depending on processing. The leftovers from the curdling process – water, milk sugar and albumen – are the whey. Commercially whey may be turned into protein additives for food products. While Miss Muffet of nursery rhyme fame ate her whey, it is not that appealing, and you will probably discard yours.

You will need to be attentive to temperature control and cleanliness throughout the process.

There are relatively inexpensive cheese making kits available to help you get started.

## Resources for Getting Started

*Home Cheese Making*
Ricki Carroll
Storey Publishing, 2002

*And That's How You Make Cheese*
Shane Sokol
iUniverse, 2001

www.cheesemaking.com (books, equipment, kits and supplies)

www.leeners.com

www.ebs.hw.ac.uk/SDA/cheese2.html

www.ext.colostate.edu/pubs/foodnut/09337.html

# CHESS

Opportunities: intellectual, social

No one is quite sure how old the game of chess is or from where it came. However, it seems likely that it was being played in India in 500 AD.

There is a story from that time period of a Hindu ruler named Sheram who was notorious for his poor management of governmental affairs. A Brahmin named Sessa taught Sheram how to play chess – then called *chaturanga* – and showed him how the game demonstrated the need to depend on others (everyone adds value, not just the king).

Eager to repay Sessa for this important lesson, Sheram asked him to choose his own reward. Sessa asked for some grains of wheat to be placed on each of the 64 squares of the chess board: one grain on the first square, two on the second square, four on the third square, eight on the fourth square, etc., doubling the number of grains on each successive square until the last square was filled.

Sheram smugly thought he was getting off cheap until it was computed that the number of grains of wheat needed to fulfill his obligation totaled 18,446,744,073,709,600,000. Another lesson learned.

A variety of Egyptian, Indian and Chinese board games predate the Indian game of 500 AD and may have had influence in its design. And a number of variations in the game have occurred over the last 1500 years. The modern game has been existence since about the 15th century.

The current general design of chess pieces dates to the mid-1800s when a British champion and editor of a newspaper chess column, Howard Staunton, endorsed a chess set design by Nathaniel Cook. Staunton also organized the first international chess tournament in 1851.

Just what is chess? It is a board game of (initially) equal opposing forces headed by Kings in which two players take turns seeking to obtain strategic advantage over the other. The ultimate objective is to position your forces in such a fashion that the opponent King is doomed.

You attack and defend, develop strategy and tactics. You can capture and regain pieces. It is an easy game to learn (there is more to it than checkers, but not so much that it is off-putting); it is inexpensive; it is very portable; it is fun for all ages; you can play against people or computers; there are chess clubs to join; you can study chess problems on your own or with others; there is always more to learn. And if you've fantasized about having bishops, knights and a queen at your command, well, you can have that too.

## Resources for Getting Started

*Complete Book of Beginning Chess*
Raymond Keene
Cardoza Publishing, 2003

*The Complete Idiot's Guide to Chess*
Patrick Wolff
Alpha Books, 2002

www.princeton.edu/~jedwards/cif/intro.html (basic instruction)

www.freechess.org
(free Internet chess server)

# CHURCH / SYNAGOGUE / MOSQUE ———

(See Religion.)

# CIVIL WAR ————————————

Opportunities: intellectual, social

Battle Hymn of the Republic vs. Dixie. Preservation of the union vs. the right to secede. Slavery as a moral issue. Slavery as an economic issue. Preservation of southern antebellum culture. The nature of our democracy. Political power. The Civil War was fought to resolve a number of issues. After four years and more than 600,000 dead, we had the answers.

For many, the fascination of this war is trying to answer the question: Why did we do this to ourselves? Over 50,000 books have been written to try to answer this question or to document or review other aspects of the conflict.

There are many ways to study the only war in which Americans fought among themselves, e.g., the battlefields, the personalities (political, military, economic), the documents and speeches, the economics of cotton, the clash of cultures, the songs, the weapons, the photographs, the aftermath.

So much written and printed material is available and so many sites have been preserved, that you can make a serious study from your home or library, and/or visit major sites related to the war — walk the battlefields, visit forts, cemeteries, museums and monuments. You might also participate in battle reenactments that are held from time to time.

## Resources for Getting Started

*Encyclopedia of the American Civil War: A Political, Social and Military History*
David Heidler (Editor) et al.
W. W. Norton & Co., 2002

*Battle Cry of Freedom: The American Civil War Era*
James M. Mc Pherson
Oxford University Press, 2003

*Fields of Fury: The American Civil War*
James M. McPherson
Atheneum, 2002

www.civilwar.com (good timeline and other info)

www.americancivilwar.com (maps, personality profiles, documents, links)

www.sunsite.utk.edu/civil-war/warweb (lots of links)

# CLASSMATES

Opportunities: social

Ever wonder what happened to_____, your best friend in the eighth grade, your senior class president, the prom queen, the person voted "most likely to succeed," the kid you used to ride the bus with, the jock, the _____ (fill in the blank)? What kind of career did she/he have? Did he/she build a family? Where does he/she live? Is he/she, in fact, alive? Did she ever get to sail to Tahiti like she always said she wanted to? Did he ever learn to fly, as he wanted to? The odds are favorable that you can find out. And perhaps you may also want to let them know what happened with you.

> **Note:** A word of caution. If you think you might like to search out someone with whom you shared a romantic interest, you might consider first and at length the sensitivities of persons close to you and the person you may be seeking.

## Resources for Getting Started

Your school's alumni relations or administration office.

Participate in a reunion.

Enter the person's name in your favorite search engine and see what pops up.

Various Internet Service Providers provide access to various "people search services" — some free, some not so free.

Specialized services like classmates.com or schoolnews.com can assist for a fee.

www.classmates.com
www.schoolnews.com

# CLIMBING

Opportunities: social, physical

"Climb every mountain . . . " Well, maybe just a few. And maybe a few interior walls.

The climbing referred to here is essentially rock climbing. Please distinguish it from, say, a hike up Mount Washington (a worthy, but quite different endeavor).

Rock climbing can literally take you places few others have gone. You can climb "big walls" that may take several days to ascend or ten-foot high boulders. You can climb ice, buildings, alpine peaks or walls built for that purpose in climbing gyms.

Why do this? You can climb for personal achievement, competition, fun, exercise, communion with nature or whatever combination gets your motor running.

Think you are too old, creaky, out-of-shape to do this? That could very well be the case! While there are "older" climbers, you need to make a very clear-headed, fact-based assessment about whether rock climbing is right for you. This activity is inherently dangerous even with safety equipment. Begin small, get instruction, take prudent safety precautions, and don't do it alone.

## Resources for Getting Started

*Complete Guide to Rock Climbing (Practical Handbook)*
Malcolm Creasey, Nigel Shepherd, Nick Banks
Lorenz Books. 2001

*The Climber's Handbook*
Garth Hattingh
Stackpole Books, 1998

www.climbing.about.com

www.onlineclimbing.com (climbing sites and gyms)

www.rockclimbing.com

# CLOCK MAKING

Opportunities: intellectual

Clocks have come a long way since someone stuck an obelisk in the ground and noted how the movement of its shadow could be used to mark the passage of time. In fact the moving shadow is what gave us the direction of "clockwise," that is, the shadow moved from the west in the morning to the east in the afternoon (from left to right if you stood south of the sundial).

When the sun went down or for cloudy days, other clocks were invented that relied on the burn rate of candles, marked reservoirs in oil lamps or the flow of water to raise a float. By the Middle Ages, oscillating clocks that relied on weights, and later springs, took over the time-telling business. Pendulums added greater accuracy. Electric power, quartz crystals and atomic clocks added more. People have been making time-keeping devices for thousands of years.

Clock Making can take you in several directions . . .

Building the clock cabinet and adding a time-keeping mechanism built by someone else;

Building a time-keeping mechanism;

A combination of the above two items;

Repair of time-keeping mechanisms;

Sitting out in your backyard on a sunny day with a good book, liquid refreshment, a piece of white cardboard, a stick and a pencil and constructing a sundial.

## Resources for Getting Started

*Clock Repair Basics*
Stephen Conover
Clockmakers Newsletter, 1996

www.spof.gsfc.nasa.gov/stargaze/Sundial.htm
(how to make a sundial)

www.clockplans.com/index.htm
(wood mechanism clock kits)

# CLOWNING

Opportunities: intellectual, social, physical

Want the world to love you? Be a clown!

Or from another perspective, think of the smiles you (as a clown) might create at children's institutions, hospitals or homes for seniors. Or block parties, fund-raising events, birthday parties and the like.

Don't know how to be a clown? There's plenty of help available, and while many professional clowns are very talented, there are very basic routines, props and costumes that enable just about anyone to generate some smiles.

There are many role models for you to consider: Charlie Chaplin, Marcel Marceau, Emmet Kelly, Buster Keaton, Red Skelton, Abbott and Costello, Jerry Lewis, Jackie Gleason.

Clowning goes back (at least) to the street acts and farces of ancient Greece and Rome and has been part of all major cultures. Clowns were used to help audiences understand Sanskrit dramas. Shakespeare used clowns in his plays. Medieval courts had their jesters. Hopi Indians used clowns in their sacred ceremonies. Circus clowns have been entertaining us since at least the 1700s. Reflect a bit on modern media and you can probably identify a number of clowns (intentional or otherwise) to add to the list.

The point here, though, is to help folks laugh by being clumsy, silly, confused, foolish, comedic, or whatever works. You get to wear funny costumes, tons of make-up, a light-up nose, a water-shooting lapel flower, an arrow through your head or none of those. You can be a mimic or a mime or both. Many options are open to you.

## Resources for Getting Started

*Clown Act Omnibus: Everything You Need to Know About Clowning Plus over 200 Clown Stunts*
Wes McVicar
Meriwether Publishing, 1987

*Creative Clowning*
Bruce Fife et al.
Piccadilly Books, 1992

*Professional organizations:*

www.coai.org

www.worldclownassociation.com

*Supplies:*

www.clownantics.com

www.clownsupplies.com

(See also Acting, Juggling, Magic, and Volunteering.)

# COIN COLLECTING

Opportunities: intellectual, social (if you wish)

Coins have been produced for over 2,500 years. The earliest were made from a material called electrum – an alloy of gold and silver – and were produced in what is now western Turkey. King Croesus of Lydia soon began minting coins of pure gold and silver and was probably a collector of sorts himself. The Greeks followed the King's lead, raised the quality of the engraving and Alexander the Great took the concept with him as he conquered much of the known (to the Greeks) world.

Collecting coins can be a fun hobby. There is much you can learn and it can be fun to build a collection, while perhaps speculating where coins have been and who might have touched them. There are also coin shows and conventions you can attend.

Collecting can be a good investment. Since, in most cases, there is a fixed number of coins of a certain type or period produced, quality examples in collections can grow in value as their brethren become lost, recycled, worn, etc.

You can approach collecting casually, simply looking through the change that passes through your hands and perhaps assembling collections of the quarters honoring each of the fifty states. Or you can approach it with varying degrees of seriousness in terms of both the time and money you allocate to it.

Many serious collectors tend to specialize, e.g. U.S. coins, foreign coins, coins from a certain period or mint.

Note: If you think you may want to approach coin collecting seriously, it is wise to "read the book before you buy" the coin. Visit your library for books on collecting and coin valuation and/or the web sites below to learn more before you begin to make "serious" investments.

## Resources for Getting Started

www.money.org (American Numismatic Association)

www.amnumsoc.org (American Numismatic Society)

www.usmint.gov

# COLLECTING —————————————————————

Opportunities: intellectual, social

People collect all sorts of stuff: art, baseball cards, coins, stamps, sea shells for sure, but also hair pins, door knobs, beer cans and barbed wire.

Why collect? It could be the pride of owning a fine assemblage of _____ (fill in the blank), a desire to build something very special or unique, or simply the thrill of the hunt followed by the display of the trophies. All that is needed is a collecting mindset and a subject matter of interest to you.

While some of these collectibles, such as coins, shells and stamps, for example, are discussed elsewhere in this text, the purpose here is simply to get your mind going (and maybe your collection started).

You can easily see, as you review the forthcoming examples of collectibles, how each of these items can also have a variety of subsets. "Tools," for example, could be hand or power, metal or wood working, shop or garden as they are used in a particular industry; or they could be from a particular manufacturer, time period or country.

Further, collecting can be something you do on your own or in collaboration with others. Certainly as you get to know other collectors, participate in clubs or attend auctions, garage sales, flea markets or conventions, you'll have many opportunities for socialization.

While the list of collectibles is as unlimited as the human imagination, the following partial list may be of help to you.

## Resources for Getting Started

*Autographs*: historical figures, entertainers, sports figures, politicians, musicians. www.autographcollector.com

*Barbed wire* (There are many types of wire.) www.barbwiremuseum.com

*Baskets*: straw, wicker, bar, wooden. www.basketmakers.com/topics/collect/collectmenu.htm

*Bells*: metal, glass ceramic, school, house, religious, musical, dinner, et al. (Pick them all or a subset.) www.americanbell.org

*Books*: rare, first editions, signed, books about particular persons, places or subjects. www.tappinbookmine.com

*Bottles*: antique, colored glass, medicine, whiskey, wine, miniatures, etc. www.fohbc.com

*Buttons:* uniform, antique, painted, wooden, stone, glass, pearl, animals, sports. www.iwantbuttons.com/NBS

*Calculators*: purely mechanical, electro-mechanical, handhelds. www.vintagecalculators.com

*Cameras*: antique, still, movie, spy, instant, large format, wooden. www.antiquewoodcameras.com/links.htm

*Clocks*: wind up, weight-driven, wood, brass. www.nawcc.org

*Clothing* (Certainly less expensive than collecting sports cars or fine art.)

*Coffee Grinders*: glass, wood, steel, wall-hung.

*Coins* (See also Coin Collection.)

*Coin-operated Machines*: penny arcade machines, old slots.

*Comic Art Forms*: art work, comic books. www.comicbooks.about.com

*Computers* (My TI still works and must be worth something!).

*Cuff Links*: historical, patriotic, gambling, financial, animals, enamel, cast. www.enamelcufflinks.com

*Kovels' Guide to Selling, Buying, and Fixing Your Antiques and Collectibles*
Ralph and Terry Kovel
Crown Trade Paperbacks
New York, New York, 1995
(an excellent book on collecting)

(See also Appendix C for a more complete collectible list.)

(See also Auctions.)
(Also on the Internet: Search for "collect"
followed by your item of interest)

## COMMUNITY SERVICE CLUBS

Opportunities: intellectual, social, perhaps more

Membership and active participation in a community service club or organization can benefit you personally as well as your community. Most will provide the opportunity for satisfaction from:

Accomplishing something worthwhile e.g. helping your community or the environment; raising money for scholarships, community parks, playgrounds, senior citizen programs and medical care for those in need;

Meeting new people;

Making friends; and

Learning new skills, etc.

While there are a variety of national organizations – some are listed below – there are also thousands of local or regional organizations. Look in your "yellow pages" or type your area of interest and location into your web browser.

Some of the clubs that have a significant "fraternal" aspect to them,, and they may have some membership requirements, e.g. being recommended by a current member, being a US citizen or of a minimum age. These are not usually burdensome.

Ever wonder what the Elks, Kiwanis, Lions, Moose and Rotarians do? Read on . . .

*The Benevolent and Protective Order of the Elks Of the USA* (BPO Elks) – The BPO Elks dates its founding to 1868 in New York City. Today its nearly 1.2 million men and women are organized into Lodges in almost 2,200 communities. They are involved in a wide range of charitable and patriotic activities with particular focus on youth, patriotic and disaster recovery programs. They support scouting, scholarships, 4-H clubs, youth athletics, drug awareness, veterans, Flag Day and civic pride programs among others. Their web site is www.elks.org

*Kiwanis International* – "Serving the Children of the World" is a major theme of the Kiwanis. Their motto is "We build." The name "Kiwanis" was adapted from an Otchipew (Native American) term "Nunc Kee-wanis" meaning, inter alia, "We make a noise." Kiwanis Club service projects focus on a wide variety of areas with a particular focus on young children. Programs for children can address needs in pediatric trauma, safety, health care, nutrition, iodine deficiency disorders, development and other areas. Other Kiwanis programs focus on the broader needs of the community including substance abuse prevention, elder care, youth sports programs, literacy and disaster response among others. Their web site is www.Kiwanis.org.

*Lions Clubs International* – "We serve" is the stated mission of the Lions Clubs International. There are more than 44,000 clubs. The organization was founded in 1917 in Illinois by a group of business organizations, which agreed that community service should be an important part of their activities. While Lions Clubs have community service programs in a wide variety of areas, they are known in particular for their service to the blind and visually impaired. In 1925, Helen Keller challenged the Lions to be "knights of the blind in the crusade against darkness." The Lions Clubs have responded with a number of programs to assist the visually challenged including recycling of eyeglasses, financial support for individuals who require cataract surgery and educational programs on diabetic eye disease and glaucoma. Other Lions Clubs activities include providing assistance to the hearing impaired, diabetes awareness and education materials, environmental projects and youth programs. Their web site is www.lionsclubs.org.

*Moose International* – Moose International is composed of two main units: the Loyal Order of Moose (for men) and the Women of the Moose (not for men). The organization was founded in the late 1800's and was originally a social institution for men. A women's organization was added early in the 1900's. Today the combined organizations have approximately 1.6 million members organized into 2,000 Lodges (men) and 1,600 Chapters (women) throughout the United States, Canada, Great Britain and Bermuda. Further, Moose International owns and operates Mooseheart, a home and school in Illinois for children in need as well as Moosehaven in Florida for Moose men and women of retirement age. While continuing to provide a fraternal environment, Moose International is involved in a wide variety of other community service activities. Their web site is www.mooseintl.org.

*Rotary International* – "Service Above Self" is the Rotary motto. There are more than 30,000 Rotary Clubs in more than 106 countries worldwide. The name "Rotary" come from the fact that the initial meetings of the organization in the early 1900's would "rotate" among members' homes. Rotarians have been a major force in the elimination of polio worldwide, both through fund-raising and through volunteers who have assisted in immunization efforts. Other Rotary efforts are directed at children's issues, poverty, hunger, improving literacy, reducing violence and promoting world understanding through international humanitarian service programs and educational and cultural exchanges. Their web site is www.rotary.org.

What if you can't find an organization that meets your needs? If you can find several other folks with a similar interest(s), you could be the catalyst for bringing them together. This could result in an informal *ad hoc* collaborative effort or perhaps it could bring together an ongoing organization with bylaws, officers, annual plan, a budget, fund-raising, and maybe even a convention!

## Resources for Getting Started

Need help in getting your fledgling organization organized? Using your computer, type "organizing a club" into your browser to see how other folks have done it, or visit your local library for a book on the topic.

*Organizations, Clubs, Action Groups: How To Start Them, How to Run Them*
Elsie E. Wolfers and Virginia B. Evansen
St. Martin's Press, 1980

# COMPOSING

Opportunities: intellectual

"All music is rehash. There are only a few notes. Just variations on a theme."

—John Lennon

You may or may not agree with Mr. Lennon's view, but it is certainly true there are a limited number of notes. And yet new songs are written every day. Why not by you?

A musical composition is essentially a melody that is played or hummed with a certain rhythm. You could hum a little ditty while reading this . . . See how easy it is? Now add lyrics and you have a song. Add chords for harmony and maybe you'll be heading to the recording studio!

It is, of course, very helpful if you have some knowledge of music; while rules do get broken in the creative process, some things do work better than others in the world of music. And it is important to be able to write down what you compose so it doesn't get lost. But what if you don't know music . . . You can do what Elvis Presley did with *Love Me Tender* — put new lyrics on the music from another song, *Aura Lee.* Or you could write a rap song where all you need is a lyric and a simple rhythm. (The author can point to raps written to celebrate a holiday and a testimonial to a college professor.)

## Resources for Getting Started

*How to Write Songs on Guitar*
Rikky Rooksby
Backbeat Books, 2000

*Melody in Songwriting*
Jack Perricone
Berklee, 2000

www.epinions.com/content_2483855492

(See also Music.)

## COMPUTERS

Opportunities: intellectual, social

Computers have become almost as ubiquitous as TVs and telephones. While the author assumes that most readers have some familiarity with computers, there are certainly some who do not. Those of you whose fingers have not yet graced a computer keyboard or swiveled a mouse on a pad are encouraged to make the time to learn. You don't need to know how to type; it is less complicated than a videocassette recorder; and it can do so much for you . . .

Letter and document preparation and storage;

Data storage;

Electronic messaging all over the world;

Music — it can bring it to you and store it for you;

Photos — storage, mailing and printing;

Research on your favorite topics or new areas of interest;

Shopping.

## Resources for Getting Started

*Absolute Beginner's Guide to Computer Basics*
Michael Miller
Cue, 2002

*PCs for Dummies*
Dan Gookin
For Dummies, 2003

# CONCERTS ─────────────────────

Opportunities: intellectual, social

If you enjoy music, why not treat yourself to a live performance? If there is a dearth of commercial venues in your area, you might consider school concerts — elementary school level can be a bit of a strain but high school and college presentations can be quite good. Look at what your area has to offer via your newspaper and local television station.

# CONDOMINIUM ASSOCIATIONS ──────

Opportunities: intellectual, social

Condominium associations exist to provide for the welfare of the property owners and to preserve the value of their property. This requires good governance by members and good management of managers, vendors, lawyers, insurance programs and accounting. It is your property; you might consider getting personally involved to help produce the best possible outcome.

## Resources for Getting Started

*The Homeowners Association Manual*
Peter Dunbar, Marc Dunbar
Pineapple Press, 2004

www.condolawyers.com

# CONGRESS

Opportunities: intellectual

They spend endless hours on minor items. They avoid dealing with issues that are screaming for attention. They spend other people's money (ours) like crazy on bridges to nowhere and rain forests in Iowa. They act based on political expediency rather than principle. Their districts are drawn to support their reelection yet they need ever-greater contributions for their campaign war chests. They vote for legislation without having read it. They talk endlessly of politics (winning and losing) and rarely of statesmanship (wisdom and acting wisely in public affairs).

That's my view. What's yours? Write to your congressperson!

## Resources for Getting Started

*Senate:*

Senator's name
Senate Office Building
Washington, DC 20510
www.senate.gov/general/contact_information/
senators_cfm.cfm

*House of Representatives:*

Representative's name
United States House of Representatives
Washington, DC 20515
www.house.gov/writerep

# CONSERVATION ——————————————————

Opportunities: intellectual, social

While cockroaches have occupied the earth far longer than we have and ants outnumber us at least a million to one, humankind is clearly the dominant species in terms of world impact.

If you think it is important that humans learn to live in greater harmony with nature, if you believe the biodiversity of plants and animals is important to the health of the planet including humankind, if you think it is important to preserve wildlife, wild lands and wetlands, you might consider learning about and becoming involved with conservation and/or preservation efforts. What's the difference? "Conservation" implies management of the biosphere to maintain its health and diversity while taking into account social and economic constraints and the needs of humans. "Preservation" implies protecting the biosphere as is without concern for other constraints or needs.

## Resources for Getting Started

*A Primer of Conservation Biology*
Richard Primack
Sinaur Associates, 2004

*The Future of Life*
Edwin Wilson
Vintage, 2003


www.nature.org/volunteer (Nature Conservancy)

www.nrcs.usda.gov (US Dept of Agriculture)

www.conservation.org (Conservation International)

(See also Environmentalism.)

---

# COOKING

Opportunities: intellectual, social, physical

You've got to eat, which means someone has to do the cooking. Now you may have been cooking all your life or perhaps someone else has done most of the cooking for you. The idea of this section is to do it a bit differently.

If you have not cooked and someone else has, offer to take over one or two nights a week. It will probably be greatly appreciated and you'll have the opportunity to learn something new.

If you have been the cook, drop some hints re: the prior paragraph and, for yourself, try some new things – not just a new recipe but new ingredients, new spices, new cooking methods, e.g. using a wok, a tagine, a steamer, slow cooker or a panini grill.

Try some ethnic cooking, e.g. Cajun, Caribbean, Chinese, Greek, Indian, Italian, Mexican, Middle Eastern, Moroccan, Spanish.

When you travel to a different region or country, try the meals new to you and see if you might like to replicate them at home.

If you have friends who enjoy cooking and trying new things, consider forming a gourmet club. You can also take cooking classes at culinary institutes, some restaurants or when you travel. (Great excuse to visit Tuscany!)

## Resources for Getting Started

Thousands of books and web sites can give you ideas, but to recommend one book and one web site, it will have to be:

*The Silver Spoon*
Phaidon Press, 2005

www.homeandfamilynetwork.com/food/ethnic.html

# COSMOLOGY ———————————————————

Opportunities: intellectual

Cosmology is the study of the origin, evolution and ultimate fate of the Universe. Where did we come from? Where are we going? How did it begin?

Think Big Bang, formation of the elements, birth of stars and galaxies, quasars, supernovae, dark matter, dark energy, formation of our solar system, black holes.

How does it all end? Or does it? Does it burn out? Does it get renewed? Are there parallel universes? Is antimatter real?

This can be a very interesting area of study and you don't need to be an astrophysicist or mathematician to get involved or have an opinion. Much of cosmology is based on theories that have yet to be proven, so you can have your own even if they disagree with that of the wiz kids. But the wiz kids have developed a lot of stuff to chew on, and it is worthwhile to spend more a bit of time reviewing their thinking. Meanwhile, the history of how this thinking developed (and changed over time) can be fascinating.

## Resources for Getting Started

*The Illustrated Theory of Everything*
Stephen W. Hawking
New Millennium Press, 2003

www.map.gsfc.nasa.gov/m_uni.html

www.astro.ucla.edu/~wright/cosmolog.htm

# COUPONS

Opportunities: intellectual

If you are like most retirees, your income is probably less than it was when you were working. While this book is not about financing your retirement, one activity you can undertake that can also be financially rewarding is the use of coupons.

Check on which days your local markets and pharmacies run ads in your newspaper and be sure to purchase the paper on those days. Also check the Sunday paper for both store and manufacturers' ads. In addition, check for any in-store specials that do not require a coupon. Clip the coupons and note the specials for items your household uses. Be sure to check for opportunities to double your coupons offered by stores.

Some stores require you have a special card to access some savings. Some of these cards can also generate additional coupons.

All of this can add up to a significant savings. Depending on your household budget, this could be in the hundreds of dollars or more every year.

It is also important that you not let yourself get carried away by purchasing items that are a "great deal" but which your household does not normally use.

## Resources for Getting Started

*Cut It Out and Start Saving*
Denise Long, Phyllis Miland
iUniverse, 2007

Greatest Secrets of the Coupon Mom
Stephanie Nelson
DPL Press, 2005

www.ultimatecoupons.com

# CROCHETING

Opportunities: physical, social

Afghans, ponchos, baby clothes, shawls, scarves, coasters, potholders — the list is quite extensive of what you can make with a continuous strand of yarn and a hook.

You can learn to do this fairly easily from some of the resources listed below as well as classes that may be available from recreation centers, adult education programs, and religious institutions. The resulting products can be used by you or make fine gifts for family, friends or for charity.

Crocheting is also one of those activities that you can do while watching TV, while with friends or while traveling (if you are not driving).

Men can do this too.

## Resources for Getting Started

*Teach Yourself Visually Crocheting*
Kim Werker, Cecily Keim
Visual, 2006

*Crocheting School*
Sterling Publishing, 2004

www.crochet.org/lessons/lesson.html

(See also Knitting.)

# ———— CROSS-COUNTRY SKIING

Opportunities: physical, social

Hint: Start with a small country! But to be serious . . .

Perhaps you have never skied. Or perhaps you have been an alpine skier and have tired of the hazards of crowds, ice, rocks, trees and snowboarders. Whatever your background, if you would enjoy an outdoor winter activity that can range from gentle and easy-going to one of the most aerobic available, that can be done anywhere there is snow (back yards, golf courses, parks, woods), you're in business. It is relatively easy to learn and relatively affordable (more than snowshoes but less than Alpine skiing). So, do consider cross-country (or Nordic) skiing.

Cross-Country is the original form of skiing, predating downhill skis by several thousand years. The necessary equipment (which can be rented) consists of skis, boots, bindings to hold your boots to your skis and poles. Unlike in Alpine skiing (where the entire boot is attached to the ski), in cross-country only the toe is attached. The free heel makes it easier to provide your own propulsion and even go uphill if you desire.

The best way to learn is to go to a Cross-Country ski center, rent equipment and take a lesson on a groomed field (groomed fields and trails are the easiest for skiing).

## Resources for Getting Started

*Cross-Country Skiing for Everyone*
James Older
Stackpole Books, 1998

*The Essential Cross-Country Skier*
Rick Lovett, Paul Peterson
International Marine, 1999

www.xcskiworld.com/beginners.htm#equipment (info for beginners)

www.xcski.org (listing of ski areas and other information)

# CROSSWORD PUZZLES ─────────

Opportunities: intellectual, possibly social

One of the author's favorite pastimes is going for a walk around the local reservoir with his spouse and a crossword puzzle book. The walk is about four miles and that is just enough time to complete a puzzle. (When we REALLY want to multi-task we also chew gum.)

Crossword puzzles are everywhere: newspapers, magazines, books, professional journals, on the web. They can be general or specialized (religious, educational, professional, pets, sports, hobbies, foreign language, travel-oriented, etc.). They can challenge your thinking and memory and help you learn new words, new uses for words and new areas to explore. You can do them on your own or in collaboration, all in one sitting or over several days, while traveling or going nowhere, in the office, in bed or on the beach.

If you really get into them, perhaps you'd enjoy creating your own, perhaps based around your family, profession, town, avocation or other area of interest. There are books and tools on the web to help you.

And to demonstrate that even crosswords can be reinvented, consider Sudoku which is from Japan (although the concept is much older) and is short for *suji wa dolushin ni kagiru* or "only single numbers are allowed." In Sudoku, you are given a nine by nine square grid that is sub-divided into nine three by three square grids. The numbers 1-9 need to be filled into each of the rows and columns of the large grid and each of the smaller grids with each number being used only once. The puzzle designer has filled in some of the numbers. You need to find the rest. It is addictive.

## Resources for Getting Started

*The New York Times Quick Crosswords:*
*Fast and Easy Puzzles*
Will Shortz, Ed.
St. Martin's Griffin, 2004

*The New York Times Ultimate Crossword Omnibus*
Will Shortz, Ed.
St. Martin's Griffin, 2003

*Sudoku Easy to Hard*
Will Shortz
St. Martin's Griffin, 2005

www.crosswordpuzzlegames.com (30,000+ puzzles)

www.crossword-puzzles.co.uk (lots of links to other puzzle sites)

www.crosswordtournament.com/links/index.htm (lots of useful links)

# CRUISES

Opportunities: intellectual, social

Many people have been on vacation cruises. But since we are retired, more or less, life seems more like one big vacation. So why go on a cruise? To eat? Gamble? Dance? See the islands? Perhaps.

How about education and adventure? Consider trips on the Nile, the Yangtze, in the Greek Islands, Norwegian Fjords, the Netherlands' canals, the Danube, the Rhine, the Galapagos, Patagonia, the Amazon, Antarctica.

## Resources for Getting Started

Cruise Lines International Association — The official trade organization of the cruise industry of North America. www.cruising.org

Grand Circle Travel
Phone: (800) 959-0405
www.gct.com

(See also Travel.)

# DANCING

Opportunities: intellectual, social, physical

"When someone blunders, we say that he makes a misstep. Is it then not clear that all the ills of mankind, all the tragic misfortunes that fill our history books, all the political blunders, all the failures of the great leaders have arisen merely from a lack of skill in dancing."

—Moliere

Humans have been dancing since we became social. The reasons for doing so are myriad, including (in more ancient times) success in hunting, end to the winter, bountiful harvests, preparation for or success in conflict, worship, the need for rain, health, romance, fertility, marriage, tribal bonding and (more recently) socialization, recreation, cultural studies, entertainment and physical fitness. But whatever the reason, we've got rhythm!

We dance alone, with another person, with other couples and with larger groups and, depending on our moods and reasons for dancing, there are scores of dance forms available to us. A few of these are referenced here to get your thinking started. If your interest is piqued, there are references for more dance forms.

**Ballroom dancing** – Remember dance class? "I saw you across the room, and I had to know you" was your paramount thought. Maybe you just got through it; maybe you learned to do it well; but the Foxtrot, Waltz, Quickstep, Tango, Cha Cha and Rumba are all calling you.

## Resources for Getting Started

*Shall We Dance? A Beginner's Guide to Ballroom Dancing*
Eric Zimmerer
Ace of Hearts, 2003

www.usabda.org (good information to help you get started)

www.ballroomdancers.com (video lessons and lots of other help)

**Belly dancing** — Pardon me, if I digress, but it can be fun. While some muscles don't get worked all that often, still you might want to try and exercise them, though perhaps not in public!

## Resources for Getting Started

*Belly Dancing Basics*
Laura Cooper, Sarah Skinner
Sterling, 2004

www.learn-to-belly-dance.com

**Ethnic dances** — Generally speaking, these are used to perpetuate custom and culture. They may frequently be done in cultural costume and be used in ethnic celebrations, e.g., the Chinese Dragon Dance, Greek Trata, the Hora, Classical Indian, Hula, Irish Step Dancing, Flamenco, African, and the Polonaise. Can you learn a dance related to your heritage?

**Folk dancing** — Its roots are in ethnic dancing but it has evolved by moving to other countries, blending with other  dance forms and innovation. There are literally hundreds of folk dances with new ones being invented on a regular basis. Examples here would include the contra dance, maypole dancing, polka, square dance, two-step and Texas line dancing.

## Resources for Getting Started

*International Folk Dancing, USA*
Betty Casey
University of North Texas, 2002

**Religious dancing** – Many religions incorporate dance into their worship.

## Resources for Getting Started

*Dance Was Her Religion*
Janet Lynn Roseman
Hohm Press, 2004

**Tap dancing** – Maybe you'd like to learn to dance like Fred Astaire and Ginger Rogers of old black and white Hollywood films.

## Resources for Getting Started

*The Souls of Your Feet*
Acia Gray
Grandweaver's Publishing, 1998

www.tapdance.org

# DARTS

Opportunities: social, physical

Darts comes from an old English word — "dhart" — for spear.

The game is said to have been developed by British soldiers in the Middle Ages who, for amusement and friendly competition, threw arrows into the ends of wine barrels to see who could come closest to the center. The wine barrel evolved into a cross section of a tree, the rings of which could help determine who had the best throw. As the cross section dried out, radial cracks appeared and the modern dartboard was invented. All that remained was to standardize the dart shaft length, determine the throwing distance from the board (four beer barrels did nicely) and set down some rules. British soldiers took the game with them around the world. It is even said that the pilgrims played darts on the Mayflower. Now darts is even the basis for a show on ESPN.

You can play in your home, by yourself or with others, in your favorite pub or in formal competition. The equipment is easy to obtain and not expensive (unless you really, really need to have tungsten tips), you don't need a lot of space, and a beer might even enhance your play. Ain't life grand?

## Resources for Getting Started

American Darts Organization, Inc.
230 N. Crescent Way #K
Anaheim, CA 92801

www.cyberdarts.com

www.dartswdf.com

# DECLUTTER

Opportunities: physical

Many of us have too much stuff. Too much stuff takes up space, weighs you down, closes you in, gets in the way (sometimes literally tripping you) and is not appreciated by your heirs. Keep the good stuff, make room for new stuff and free up your life by decluttering:

Attics

Basements

Bookshelves

Cars

Closets

Computer files

Desks

Drawers

Gadgets

Garages

Magazine stacks

Medicine cabinets

Workshops

What to do with it all? Sell it, if possible. Gift it, if you can't sell it. (Nursing homes might like books; The Salvation Army or Goodwill Industries might value clothing and you get a tax deduction.). Recycle it if you can't give it away (your stuff gets a new life). Toss it, if all else fails.

## Resources for Getting Started

*Clear Your Clutter with Feng Shui*
Karen Kingston
Broadway, 1999

*Let Go of Clutter*
Harriet Schecter
McGraw-Hill, 2000

www.organizedhome.com/content-2.html

www.freecycle.com

# DECORATIVE ARTS ────────────

Opportunities: intellectual, social

Look around you. Could your living or work space use some brightening up or embellishment? Might it be fun to personalize some everyday objects? Might it be fun to make some decorative/functional items for friends, family or fund-raising events?

Can you work with paper, glue, scissors, paint, pencils, craft knives and the like? Can you trace designs from design books (available in your library)? If you answered, "Yes," consider making:

*Appliqué* (applying a cut-out, say cloth or paper, to a larger surface) : You probably made Valentines this way in grammar school. You might use appliqué with . . .

Blankets

Book covers

Clothing

Curtains

Greeting cards

Lampshades

Napkins

Pillow

Postcards

Quilts

Tablecloths

Ceramic tiles painted for your bathroom or kitchen: you need tiles, ceramic paint, a design(s) and an oven to bake the tiles.

*Découpage* (paper designs glued onto objects, sometimes sealed with varnish or lacquer): Items to which you might apply decoupage . . .

Boxes

Bowls

Cabinets

Clocks

Door plates

Lamps

Furniture

Picture frames

Placemats

Plant pots

Plates

Trays

Umbrella stands

Walls

Wastebaskets

Game table (chess, checker, backgammon): wooden fold-up TV tray, paint and varnish.

*Gilded candlesticks* (Don't have a lily?): wooden candles sticks, paint and gilt cream or gold paint.

*Hooked rug*: buy a kit (a good way to start) or make your own design.

*Mosaic table*: you need a table base, wooden table top, a mosaic design (make you own or use a design book), ceramic tiles, tile cutters and grout and lead strip edging.

*Mosaic mirror frame*: as above but with a mirror frame.

*Painted flower pot*: terra cotta pot, ceramic paint and design (stripes, zigzags, spots, something more elaborate).

*Painted glass bottles*: glass bottles, glass paint.

*Painted wooden planter*: planter, paint and design.

*Stenciled furniture*: wood furniture, paint stencil design.

*Stenciled peg coat hanger*: wooden hanger, stencil design, paint.

*Watering can*: steel can and paint.

There are many other items to which you can apply your creative talents and a wide variety of mediums you can use in the process.

## Resources for Getting Started

*Complete Home Crafts*
Miranda Innes
DK Publishing, Inc, 1997

*Complete Craft: Making Beautiful Projects at Home*
Katherine Sorrell, Howard Sooley
Thunder Bay Press, 2003

www.creativity-portal.com/howto/artscrafts/
home.decorating.html

www.theappliquesociety.org

www.decoupage.org

## DECOYS

Opportunities: intellectual, social

Reference is made here to wooden decoys — of ducks and geese — used to attract the real thing.

Duck decoys are an invention of Native Americans. The oldest known decoys date from around 1,000 AD and were made of wood, bulrushes and feathers. The Native Americans taught the European settlers how to make and use them in support of both the business and sport of water fowling. The Europeans used their more highly developed tools and stains/paints to produce very life-like decoys from blocks of wood. While synthetic materials are now used to produce decoys that are lightweight and stackable for use by water fowlers, a few traditionalists still carve and paint their own. You can too.

If you are feeling intrepid, you could start with a block of wood and carve your own (plans are available to assist you) or you can purchase a kit that does much of the preliminary work for you so you can focus on the finishing aspects. While these can be used for hunting, many folks will find they make nice decorative pieces.

Many wooden decoys were produced during the late 1800s and early 1900s. These can be interesting items for collections.

## Resources for Getting Started

*The Decorative Decoy Carver's Ultimate Painting &
Pattern Portfolio*
Bruce Burk
Fox Chapel Publishing, 2004

*Carving Decorative Duck Decoys*
Harry Shourds, Anthony Hillman
Dover Publications, 1984

www.wildfowl-carving.com

www.duxdekes.com

# DIVING (SCUBA AND SNORKELING) ——————

Opportunities: physical, intellectual, social (best not done alone)

As long as you have a healthy heart and lungs you can probably participate in scuba diving activities. The main concern in scuba is your body's ability to balance oxygen and carbon dioxide levels. A Duke University Medical Center study found that the body's ability to do that doesn't change significantly simply as a function of age.

But since you are a unique individual, it would be best to check with your physician to get a professional view on this subject. If your doctor says it is okay and you are a novice, you will probably want to get thumbs up from your doctor in writing, since many scuba instruction organizations will require it. Even with your doctor's okay, some scuba companies may decline to take you on if you have a history of elevated blood pressure or other issues. If you are planning a vacation around diving and have a potential issue, it is best to check with the dive company in advance.

If you can't scuba, you an always snorkel. And while snorkelers can't visit many wrecks or swim with the bottom-feeding fish, you can still swim *with* the fish, get to see what is under the water and if are in the right latitude or can go visit, observe the beauty of coral reefs.

## Resources for Getting Started

*The Certified Diver's Handbook*
Clay Coleman
International Marine/Ragged Mountain Press, 2004

*The Simple Guide to Snorkeling Fun*
Steven Barsky
The Best Publishing Company, 1999

www.padi.com (PADI is the Professional Association of Diving Instructors)
www.skin-diver.com (lots of educational material)

www.npca.org/marine_and_coastal/coral_reefs/
snorkeling.html

# DOCENT

Opportunities: intellectual, social

A docent is a person who leads guided tours at an art gallery, garden, museum, zoo or other venue where the visitors would benefit from having someone help them understand and appreciate what they are viewing. Other docents may provide tours of battlefields, architecture or city historical districts. While most docents are volunteers, there may be compensated positions in some settings.

You may already have sufficient knowledge to perform as a competent docent or you may need to study. Most docents find that they continue to grow in knowledge and perspective from the questions and comments of visitors. One of the most interesting docents I have met was at the Museum of Scotland in Edinburgh. He had been a successful business person and Trustee of the Museum for many years and "retired" to be a docent. His love and enthusiasm for the museum's collections just radiated from him and he noted that he learned something everyday, frequently from the many international visitors to the museum.

If being a docent sounds interesting, you might take a tour with a docent yourself and focus on what they do. After the tour see if the docent could spend a few minutes talking about being a docent, what he or she likes and doesn't like about it, how he or she became one and any advice he or she might have for someone who is thinking about entering the field.

## Resources for Getting Started

*Interpretation for the 21st Century*
Larry Beck, Ted T. Cable
Sagamore Publishing, 2002

*The Good Guide: A Sourcebook for Interpreters, Docents, and Tour Guides*
Alison L. Grinder
Ironwood Press, 1985

www.stlzoo.org/education/zoodocents/ (zoo docent)

www.sfmoma.org/info/getinv_docent.html (museum docent)

www.torreypine.org/misc/volunteering.html (park docent)

## DOGS

Opportunities: social (required), physical (if you walk and play)

Companionship, love and affection, playmate, someone to talk to, exercise companion, good Samaritan, guardian – dogs can deliver on all fronts.

But dogs also require time and attention on a daily basis (including scooping the poop); regular exercise; periodic grooming and vet care; and, if you are getting a puppy, training. You need to think carefully as to whether you are ready for the responsibility and the annual cost – probably at least five hundred dollars per year – and more for a larger dog. If a dog seems like too much to handle, please see the sections on "cats" and "pets."

Dogs are most likely descended from wolves and have a relationship (hunting, herding, guarding, companionship) with humans going back at least 14,000 years. Dogs are social creatures and need interaction with you. They are also pack animals which helps them remain effective guardians, but it also means they need to know who is the leader of the pack (hopefully that is you, not Fido).

There are at least 400 breeds of dogs from which to choose and it makes good sense to research these breeds with respect to size, exercise needs, ease of training, general personality characteristics and so forth. Your library or the American Kennel Club web site can get you started.

If you are thinking of getting a puppy, it pays to read a book on raising puppies to see what you are getting yourself into.

If you decide on a puppy, a breeder will probably be your best source – see the AKC web site for more information. Breeders may also sometimes have some older dogs that are trained but are no longer suited for breeding. Another good source for trained, older dogs can be animal shelters. Newspapers may also have ads for trained dogs that are available for adoption due to the owners change in job or housing situation.

What else can your dog do in addition to being your companion?

Play with the grandkids after they've tuckered you out.

Take you for a long walk, daily. You'll thank your dog for the expenditure of calories and fresh air (you won't be quite as thankful on rainy days but life is full of trade-offs isn't it?); your dog will thank you for all the good smells.

Go with you to visit nursing homes, assisted living facilities or hospitals. You'll be amazed at just how much happiness a three-minute visit with your Fido can bring to someone. Fido may need to be "certified" as sufficiently well behaved to do this; also check with the facility first to see if they welcome these types of visits and when is the best time to arrive (Hint: avoid meal times).

You might also consider . . .

Providing a home and house training for dogs that will ultimately assist the blind (it can be tough to let them go, though);

Working in an animal rescue program or shelter;

Becoming a breeder yourself;

Entering shows or obedience competitions;

Sending a video of your pooch to Animal Planet; and

Offering to be a pet sitter or walker.

## Resources for Getting Started

*The Complete Dog Book*
The American Kennel Club Staff
Howell Book House, 1998

*Good Dogs, Great Owners*
Brian Kilcommons, Sarah Wilson
Warner Books, 1999

*How to be your Dog's Best Friend*
The Monks of New Skete
Little, Brown, 2002

*Therapy Dogs*
Kathy Diamond Davis
Dogwise Publishing, 2002

*The Complete Book of Dog Breeding*
Dan Rice
Barron's, 1997

www.akc.org (click on the "Breeds" button)

www.dogs.about.com

## DOLL MAKING/COSTUMING ─────────────

Opportunities: intellectual

Dolls were probably the earliest form of manufactured toy. They have been made from wood, bone, straw, clay, cloth, metal, porcelain, plastic and other materials. Making dolls can be a form of artistic expression, but they also make very fine gifts for the younger folks in your life or as contributions to families who are not otherwise able to afford gifts for children. If your doll-related ambition is not sated with the basic doll, you might also consider doll costuming, doll houses, doll furniture or collecting.

### Resources for Getting Started

*Creative Cloth Doll Making*
Patti Medaris Culea
Quarry Books, 2003

*Designing the Doll*
Susanna Oroyan
C&T Publishing, 1999

(See also Puppeteering.)

## DRAW ──────────────────────────────

Opportunities: intellectual

All you need is a pencil and paper and you can become an artist. Actually it helps to learn the *craft* of drawing before you wax artistic. And drawing *is* a craft you can learn through classes and/or books or digital media. You begin with learning how to really see what it is you are going to draw and then developing skills in drawing fundamental shapes and added shading and perspective. Then you can sketch your abode, your pet, your plant, nature scenes, your neighbor, you name it.

## Resources for Getting Started

*Draw What You See*
Rudy De Reyna
Watson-Guptill, 1996

*New Drawing on the Right Side of the Brain*
Betty Edwards
Tarcher, 1999

*Pencil Drawing Techniques*
David Lewis, Ed.
Watson-Guptill, 1984

www.learn-to-draw.com

# DRIFTWOOD

Opportunities: intellectual (figuring out what
to do with it), physical (going and getting it)

Driftwood is fun stuff. You can use it in floral arrangements, for decoration as piece of nature art, for furniture, in aquariums, or just as curiosity pieces. The author has collected pieces that look amazingly like the Road Runner ("beep, beep") cartoon character and a coelacanth (ancient fish thought to be extinct for 80 million years but discovered off the coast of Africa in 1938).

You don't live near an ocean beach? No problem. You can also find pieces on lake shores (the author's pieces referenced above are lake pieces) and around dams, rivers and streams. You may even find some interesting pieces in the forest or desert where instead of being weathered by water, the wood has been affected by wind, sun and/or sandblasting.

Be sure to think about the possibilities presented by small pieces that might be removed from larger ones, e.g. removing a root from a large trunk.

If you live near a ready source and enjoy collecting, you might find that a florist might be interested in purchasing some of your finds from you.

## Resources for Getting Started

*Driftwood Sculpture*
Patricia Bartlett
Waterfront Publications, 2000

*The Driftwood Book*
Mary E. Thompson
Van Nostrand Company, 1966

# EATING

Opportunities: social, physical

While eating may seem a somewhat obvious activity in which to engage, retired or not, consider some variations on the topic . . .

*Dine-out group*: Form a group with fellow eaters to dine out together periodically with a focus on trying new restaurants.

*Ethnic dining*: Try restaurants that offer food types or preparations with which you are not familiar. If you come to like the style, you might purchase a cookbook and learn to prepare those types of meals at home.

*Healthy dining*: Eating out or at home, consider focusing on a meal that is delicious, nutritious and healthy, e.g. lean meat and fish, skinless poultry, beans, zero or low fat cooking methods, fruits and veggies, minimal salad dressing, low fat milk, reduced salt and sugar, moderate levels of alcohol.

*Best Value dining*: Rate restaurants on the value they provide you. Reward those that provide the best value with repeat business. For value, consider: meal cost, food quality, ambiance, service, convenience, parking.

*Gourmet club*: Consider forming a Gourmet Club for socialization and to try new foods and cooking styles. These clubs can operate in various ways but typically the hosting of the meal is on a rotating basis; everyone shares in the meal preparation responsibilities and the cost of food and beverages. For an example of how one club works, visit the web site below.

## Resources for Getting Started

www.indiana.edu/~uclub/gourmet.html

## EDUCATION

Opportunities: intellectual, social

*High School*: Didn't get to finish? Here's your opportunity! You can prepare for and take the General Education Development (GED) test. Passing this test shows that you have achieved high school level academic skills.

The GED has five parts: Writing, Social Studies, Science, Reading and Mathematics. Many school systems offer free classes to help you prepare for the test. There are also a wide variety of study aids and commercial tutoring programs.

Tests are administered in over 3,500 locations around the country, usually in public school buildings. Almost all colleges and universities will accept the GED in place of a high school degree.

*College*: Finish your degree or add another if you are so inclined. However, since you may not be studying for a future career, you can just take courses for the joy of learning. Many state schools allow folks of a certain age to attend classes at little or no cost.

*Lifelong Education Institutes*: These are community-based educational organizations, frequently associated with a college or university, that are focused on providing continuing educational opportunities for people of retirement age regardless of any previous levels of education.

What to study? Anything that grabs you! If you don't have an immediate particular interest, try an introductory course in an area with which you have no experience. Consider, for example, sculpting, meteorology, philosophy, Haiku, modern dance, Chinese history. You will learn something (and build some new neural connections as you do). You will probably also have fun, and you will be out and about and meeting new people.

## Resources for Getting Started

Check out High Schools and Colleges in your area.

www.elderhostel.org/ein (Lifelong Education Institutes)

www.osher.net

# EMBROIDERY

Opportunities: intellectual, social

Embroidery is needlework used to decorate clothing and household items as well as to tell a story. The use of embroidery dates back to the early Egyptians and Middle East; it was also used very early on in China, Asia and Korea. Why, our forebears may have asked, wear simple animal skins or plain textiles when you can express yourself, or show off your wealth and importance with embroidery?

Embroidery has been done with beads, shells, silk, colored thread, even thin strands of gold. Embroidering ecclesiastical vestments, altar cloths and court clothing was a high art form in the Middle Ages and Renaissance.

One of the largest pieces of handmade embroidery in existence is the more than 900-year-old Bayeaux Tapestry. At 271 feet in length, it tells the story of William the Conqueror's defeat of Harold, the Earl of Wessex at the Battle of Hastings in 1066. The original is in Bayeux, France; there is a copy in Reading, England. It may be interesting to note that the Bayeux Tapestry is not really a tapestry since a tapestry is *woven* not embroidered, but who wants to argue with the French?

Embroidery is still very popular today but much of what you see is produced by machine rather than by hand. But there is no need for you to run out and purchase an embroidery machine if the idea of embroidering your shirts, hats, jeans or other items piques your interest. You can learn to do this on your own for yourself or to produce gifts; and you may very well find someone else in your quest for the perfect pattern who loves embroidery as you have come to love it.

## Resources for Getting Started

*123 Embroidery*
Ellen Moore Johnson
Rockport Publishers, 2003

*Anchor Complete Embroidery Course*
Christina Marsh
David & Charles, 2003

www.craftown.com/instruction/embroidery.htm

# ENVIRONMENTALISM

Opportunities: intellectual, social, physical

It sometimes seems that mankind simply takes resources from the environment and puts back waste. For most of our history, the world just seemed so vast that we could get away with that approach. But as we built cities and learned the importance of clean water and the need to deal more effectively with sewage and other urban challenges, the world gradually became a smaller place. That learning process continues today as we watch rain forest depletion, species extermination and increasing pollution of air and water among other problems.

Environmentalists (that can and should be any and all of us) look at mankind's interaction with the environment and reflect on the actions we should be taking to protect our natural resources and ecosystems. It has taken us tens of thousands of years to position ourselves to wreak havoc on the planet; it will probably take centuries (at least) to bring matters into a sustainable balance.

Consider picking a topic and getting involved to help build a better world . . .

    Air quality

    Animal habitats

    Energy availability and efficiency

    Food safety

    Forest management

    Housing density

    Land restoration

    Light pollution

    Transportation availability and efficiency

    Trash management

        Reduction

        Recycling

        Composting

    Water quality

        Rain

        Streams/rivers

        Swamps

        Lakes

        Oceans

A caution: environmentalism, like many other "movements," has a lunatic fringe that is "anti" private property, big business, capitalism, technology, globalization, fossil fuels, dams, roads and many other aspects of modern life. What is needed, of course, is sound public policy based on rigorous scientific analysis and fact-based cost/benefit analyses that enable us to balance the needs of humanity with the needs of the planet. So beware of the whackos but know that you can make a difference if you get involved.

## Resources for Getting Started

*Hands-On Environmentalism*
Brent Haglund, Thomas Still
Encounter Books, 2005

*Free Market Environmentalism*
Terry Anderson, Donald Leal
Palgrave Macmillan, 2001

*Modern Environmentalism: An Introduction*
David Pepper
Routledge, 1996

(See also Conservation and Trees.)

# ESSAYS ─────────────────────────────

Opportunities: intellectual

Remember essays? Introductory (thesis) paragraph, supporting paragraphs to prove your thesis, summary/conclusion paragraph?

You probably had to do them in school, to get into college or perhaps your parents compelled you to write one or more on some aspects of your childhood behavior.

Having reached your maturity, there may be one or more essays within you waiting to be set free. You might consider aspects of politics, government, lessons from history, labor relations, product quality, social relations, the changing seasons, education, entertainment, religion, art, femininity, manhood, health, bioethics, privacy, cloning, gun control, animal rights, crime, terrorism, parenting, manners, the environment, sunrise, sunset, the meaning of life; believe me, the list is endless, if you just give it a moment's thought.

Having produced an essay, what do you do with it? Perhaps it goes in your personal journal or you may decide to attempt publication in a newspaper or magazine by sending it to the publication's editor. If hardcopy publication does not work out, you might consider web publication by means of your own blog or someone else's.

## Resources for Getting Started

www2.actden.com/writ_den/tips/essay/

www.pbs.org/newshour/essays-dialogues.html

www.goodessaytopics.com

# ESTATE PLANNING

Opportunities: intellectual, social

Sooner or later we will die. What happens then?

With respect to your estate — all of your real estate, investments and personal property — it is your call. If you do nothing, the state in which you live will place someone in charge of your estate to pay off expenses and debts and then distribute the remaining assets according to state law. If *you* prefer to direct what will happen with your estate, you need to make a plan and assure the proper documents are in place to put your plan into effect once you have come to your journey's end.

An effective estate plan will help:

Make sure your assets go where you want them to go;

Avoid inheritance squabbles;

Facilitate the distribution of assets in a timely manner;

Keep a family business functioning;

Reduce taxes.

So, how do you create an Estate Plan? The basic steps are . . .

Decide what you want to have happen with your assets. Everything to your spouse or some other individual? Distributions to various folks? Do you want to arrange for someone to manage your investments for the benefits of others? Are there particular possessions you want to leave to particular individuals? Anything to schools or charity? How about Fido?

Gather the relevant information and documents: real estate, major possessions, banking and investment accounts, insurance policies, debts, will, tax returns, pension information and the like.

Select and visit with a financial planner to go over what you want to do with what you have (including supporting yourself until it is time to step onto the Stygian ferry).

Even if you have the expertise to develop the plan yourself, it can be helpful to review everything with a professional to get a second opinion. Of course, just about anyone can dub himself or herself a financial planner; therefore, a bit of research into qualifications is in order.

Visit with an attorney who specializes in estate planning for further advice and to have the appropriate documents — will, trust(s), power of attorney — prepared.

Depending on your situation, your financial advisor and/or attorney may suggest you meet with an investment advisor, insurance professional or CPA/tax advisor.

Review your plan periodically to assure it remains current with your wishes.

## Resources for Getting Started

*AARP Crash Course in Estate Planning*
Michael Palermo
Stirling, 2002

*Your Estate Matters*
Patti Spenser
Authorhouse, 2005

www.aarp.org/money/financial_planning/sessioneight/understanding_financial_credentials.html

www.abanet.org/rppt/public (American Bar Association overview)

---

# EXERCISE

Opportunities: social, physical

This is not a book about exercise or staying fit in our older years; there are many other fine books and other resources devoted to those subjects. However, it would be remiss not to point out that exercise is the most straightforward way of being physically engaged. While many other activities in this book will engage you physically, physical engagement is the whole point of exercise. While there are many options for exercise, here are the biggies.

*Aerobic*: This is the stuff that gets your heart and lungs moving. It helps to improve the functioning of your heart and lungs, lowers blood pressure, boosts good cholesterol and reduces body fat and weight. You want a rhythmic activity that makes your heart and lungs work harder, such as:

aerobic dancing
bicycling
cross-country skiing
in-line skating
jazzercise
snowshoeing
stair climbing
swimming
walking (4+ miles per hour)

*Stretching*: Stretching increases the length of your muscles and tendons. You do this in order to increase the range of motion of your limbs and joints thus making them more "flexible." Stretching prepares your muscles and tendons to be active; without stretching you increase the risk of injury. As with weight training, it is important to learn how to stretch properly. There are a wide variety of books on this subject.

*Walking*: Simply walking out the door for 10 minutes, turning around and coming back can help with weight, blood pressure and cholesterol control, if done on a regular basis. If you can gradually work your way up to an hour-long walk at a four mile an hour pace, you can do yourself a lot of good. Be sure to stretch first and wear good shoes.

*Weight training*: This helps you build strong muscles, bones and joints. It can also help reduce blood pressure and cholesterol and improve other health dimensions. With weight training you subject your muscles to greater resistance than that to which they are accustomed and, with repetition, you build endurance. It is important that weight training be done properly and not too aggressively in order to avoid injury. Therefore, getting some professional advice is highly advisable.

## Resources for Getting Started

*Stretching*
Bob Anderson
Shelter Publications, 2000

*Somatics*
Thomas Hanna
Da Capo Press, 2004

www2.gsu.edu/~wwwfit/strength.html (info on weight training)

(See also Weightlifting and Yoga.)

# FAMILY RELATIONSHIPS

Opportunities: social

Do you have family members who have moved or grown away from you geographically, socially, economically or emotionally? Or perhaps there has been a more significant estrangement based on some event or behavior.

Consider whether you might want to begin to build a bridge to those family members. Of course, successful bridge building requires effort at both ends; it may not work. But perhaps you could be the one to reach out; and if it doesn't work, at least you'll know you tried.

## Resources for Getting Started

*Healing from Family Rifts*
Mark Siechel
McGraw-Hill, 2002

www.ehow.com/how_2299088_mend-family-rift.html

# FAMILY MEMORY BOOK———————————

Opportunities: intellectual, social

Would it be interesting and useful to assemble a book that includes information about your family? You could include a family tree; family member biographies; photographs of your family, home(s), pets and friends; information on family achievements (sports, military service, careers, education, community service, inventions and the like) and favorites (vacations, recipes, traditions, holiday celebrations, music, friends, etc). This is the kind of project that can involve all members of your family; ask them to supply the desired information for inclusion.

You could assemble this on your own in scrapbook fashion or use a commercially prepared book.

## Resources for Getting Stated

*Our Family History*
Reader's Digest Editors
Reader's Digest, 1999

# FAMILY TREE

Opportunities: intellectual, social

Researching and documenting your family tree, a genealogical diagram of who begat whom, can be both educational and fun.

I learned from a few hours research on the web that the paternal side of my family in the States dates back to 1640 and a Benjamin Price who owned land in the Hamptons on Long Island. (I do wish he had kept it in the family!) He also was part of a group that purchased Montauk Point from the Indians. Ben was originally from Wales, but I haven't been able find out where as yet. Since Ben, my paternal ancestry has included a yeoman, a cordwainer (a shoemaker), a soldier who fought on both sides of the Revolutionary War (first for the Loyalists, then for the good guys), a physician, an abolitionist, a farmer and two ministers.

You can purchase pre-printed family trees where all you have to do is fill in the blanks. You can also make your own or purchase software that will help you build one.

## Resources for Getting Started

*The Everything Family Tree Book*
Kimberly Powell
Adams Media, 2006

www.familytreesearcher.com

(See Genealogy.)

# FENCING

Opportunities: intellectual, social, physical

Ever have daydreams about being Hollywood's old-time film swashbuckling Errol Flynn? Or perhaps Richard Chamberlin in the movie *The Count of Monte Cristo*? One of the three (or four) Musketeers? Robin Hood? The Highlander? Or (making no assumptions about your gender) perhaps the more current film star Catherine Zeta-Jones parrying the thrusts of Antonio Banderas in *The Mask of Zorro*?

Sword fighting as a means of settling disputes has been around since the Bronze Age. The Greeks and Romans generally used short and wide swords; our medieval ancestors used long and heavy broadswords; the samurai and warriors in other cultures all developed their own styles of sword weapons. When we figured out how to blow each other up with gunpowder, the sword began a decline as a major weapon of choice. It became a side arm of gentlemen and then largely ceremonial (although there was a report in 1997 of a mayor of an Italian city challenging some Mafia types to a duel).

While sword fighting as a sport can be traced to the Egyptians, modern fencing really dates from the Renaissance. When the Olympic Games began again in 1896, fencing was included and it is one of only six sports to have been included in all modern Olympic competitions.

Why might you want to explore fencing? Beyond fulfillment of the fantasies listed at the beginning of this section, think: exercise, balance, agility (physical and mental), grace, self-confidence, problem solving, socialization, and competition.

Modern fencing can be very safe and good fun, if you use the appropriate protective clothing, mask and other equipment; take appropriate training at a fencing school or club; abide by fencing etiquette (part of the fun actually); and participate in supervised bouts.

## Resources for Getting Started

*The Art and Science of Fencing*
Nick Evanangelista
Masters Press, 1996

www.fencing101.com

# FENG SHUI

Opportunities: intellectual, social

Common sense would tell most people that if they have a choice of vistas from the front door of their home of either an open field, or three dead trees and a brick wall, that the open field is preferable. It would also tell you that it is generally not a good thing for your love life to hang portraits of your in-laws in sight of your matrimonial bed. Feng Shui would tell you the same things and more.

Feng Shui (pronounced Fung Schway) is Chinese for "wind plus water." Thousands of years ago, the Chinese determined that it made good sense to consider the potential impact of wind and water with respect to the selection of burial sites. From this logical underpinning, Feng Shui has grown into an art form that focuses on the design and positioning of cemeteries, buildings, gardens, furnishings and other items to be in harmony with nature. The theory seems to be that our lives are affected by our surroundings; if we go with the natural flow of things and construct peaceful and harmonious environments in which to live and work we are more likely to think positively and be happy, healthy, wealthy and possessed of good relationships. Conversely, if we construct an environment that is garish, discordant and out of step with nature, we are likely to be unhappy in a number of ways.

Some practitioners of Feng Shui believe that, as with traditional Chinese medicine, being successful with Feng Shui requires an appreciation of the flow of chi — the life force inherent in all things — and the patterns of the primal forces of yin (darker, passive, feminine) and yang (brighter, active, and masculine). Others also believe or hope that you can modify your Feng Shui environment through the use of mirrors, crystals, paper cut-outs, miniature water falls, colored dots and the like.

Basic Feng Shui seems quite rational. But first this question: do you think the ancient Dutch would have settled Holland if they had studied Feng Shui? Whether you can improve your happiness with crystals and mirrors, I leave to you.

## Resources for Getting Started

*Feng Shui Your Life*
Jayme Barrett
Stirling, 2003

*Feng Shui: Harmony by Design*
Nancy Santopietro
Perigee, 1996

www.webterrace.com/fengshui

# FINANCIAL PLANNING/INVESTING

Opportunities: intellectual

"If You Don't Know Where You're Going, You'll Probably End Up Somewhere Else."

—David Campbell

Campbell's observation is as relevant to financial planning as it is to other life choices.

The average 65-year-old person is looking at about 18 years of additional engagement. A financial plan will map out how to manage your assets to meet your goals for the rest of your life. With map in hand you then need to act on your plan and periodically revisit it to assure it remains current. There are many books and web sites (particularly those of mutual fund companies) that can provide assistance. If you lack the time or the expertise to do it on your own, financial planners can assist you. And even if you can create your own plan, it may be helpful to have a professional, ideally someone who doesn't have anything to sell you other than advice, to review your plan for completeness, realism and opportunities for improvement. As mentioned in the section on Estate Planning, just about anyone can dub themselves a financial planner; therefore, a bit of research into qualifications is appropriate.

You might consider learning more about managing your own money. Again, many of the mutual fund company web sites like Fidelity, T. Rowe Price and Vanguard can be helpful. You also might consider forming or joining an investment club as a way to learn with others. Even if you do not choose to actively manage your assets, the knowledge you gain by learning more about how to do it can be helpful for interacting with those who do it for you.

## Resources for Getting Started

*Personal Financial Planning*
G. Victor Hallman, Jerry S. Rosenbloom
McGraw-Hill, 2003

*Common Sense on Mutual Funds*
John Bogle
John Wiley & Sons, 1999

www.aarp.org/money/financial_planning/sessioneight/
understanding_financial_credentials.html

www.cfp-board.org (financial planning info)

www.aarp.org/money/financial_planning (financial planning info)

www.betterinvesting.org (investment club info)

# FISHING

Opportunities: intellectual, social, physical

The author's first recollection of fishing dates to the early 1950s: a sunny and breezeless day, a short rod, a bobber, a coffee can full of worms, a dammed pond full of catfish and "sunnies" and no one else around but my father. Fast forward to 2005 and the Abacos in The Bahamas: it is 0700 and the author is just waking up on his chartered catamaran, which is anchored off Treasure Cay. Waking at that particular moment is occasioned by the sound of multiple diesel engines passing off the port side — scores of sport fishing boats, hailing from Massachusetts to Texas, carrying multiple rods and fully equipped with bait, beer and enthusiastic anglers are heading out for the annual billfish competition. Tens of millions of dollars worth of aquatic glory chug by as I sip my coffee.

Fishing offers a wide range of experiences based on . . .

Equipment: simple pole and line fishing, spincasting, baitcasting, flyrod, saltwater rod, ice fishing "tip-up;"

Location: shore, in a river with waders, pier, beach, bridge, boat (moving or stationary), frozen surface;

Companionship: solo, best buddy or relative, commercial fishing charter;

Motivation: relaxation, fun, food, competition.

With fishing, you can spend a little money for a lot of fun and spend a boatload of money for however much fun you can make of it. The choice is yours.

In most states you will need a license for fishing in freshwater and you may need one for some forms of saltwater fishing.

## Resources for Getting Started

*What the Fish Don't Want You to Know*
Frank Baron
International Marine, 2003

*The Complete Book of Saltwater Fishing*
Milt Rosko
Kp Books, 2001

www.fishing.about.com (freshwater fishing)

www.saltfishing.about.com (saltwater fishing)

www.takemefishing.org (fishing regulations of all states plus more)

# FLY TYING

Opportunities: intellectual, physical (manual dexterity)

This is also for all you fisher-people. As you know, fish are picky. They eat what they want, which is not necessarily what you have. But if you can observe what they are eating, you can tie your own flies and coax them to your line.

## Resources for Getting Started

*The Art of Fly Tying*
Claude Chartrand
Firefly Books, 1996

*Guide Flies: How to Tie and Fish the Killer Flies from America's Greatest Guides and Fly Shops*
Dave Klausmeyer
Countryman Press, 2003

www.flytyingworld.com

www.flyfishing-and-flytying.co.uk

# FINAL PLANS

Opportunities: social (you can organize it, if you wish!)

When the time comes to joining your ancestors, there are a variety of activities that must or may be "undertaken" . . .

Disposition of your body (a must);

Funeral or memorial service (a maybe);

Publication of your obituary (a maybe);

Settlement of your estate (a must).

Various aspects of these activities may be governed or influenced by your state government, your religion or family traditions. But you also have the opportunity to express your wishes in anticipation of the event and, at the same time, make the handling of your final arrangements easier on your friends and family. You can let people know orally what your thoughts are, but it also helps if you put your wishes in writing and that you let people know where they can find the document that records your wishes.

Consider documenting your views on the following:

Cremation or burial?

If cremation, ashes scattered somewhere or retained?

If burial, where and type of casket?

If cremation, immediate or after a funeral with a viewing?

If burial, immediate or after funeral with a viewing?

If there is a service with a viewing, what would you like to be wearing?

Instead of a funeral would you prefer a memorial service at a later date?

Is there anything you would like read, said or sung at a funeral or memorial service?

If you will have a gravesite, what kind of grave marker would you like?

If you were a veteran, would you like a military marker at your gravesite?

If you have a grave marker, would you like an epitaph, and if so, what would you like your epitaph to say?

What would you like in your obituary?

To what publications or institutions would you like your obituary sent?

Beyond simply expressing your wishes, you could make many of these arrangements in advance and even pre-fund them if that seems appropriate to you. You could write your own obituary (who knows you better than you?) and your own farewell letter to be read at your funeral or service if you wish.

It would also be helpful if you could document where to find stuff: keys to the house and car, insurance policies, safe deposit box and key, will, credit cards, savings and checking accounts, CDs, stock accounts, IRAs and the like.

Any of the above actions will be greatly appreciated by those who remain a bit longer after you move on.

## Resources for Getting Started

*In the Checklist of Life*
Lynn McPhelimy
AAIP Publishing, 1997

*Everything Your Heirs Need to Know*
David S. Magee, John Ventura
Kaplan Business, 1998

www.ftc.gov/bcp/conline/pubs/services/funeral.htm (info from the Federal Trade Commission on Funerals)

www.dying.about.com

## GAMES

Opportunities: intellectual, social, physical

There are literally thousands of games with which you can have a great time with friends and which you can use to develop new friendships. The ones listed here are just to get you started in remembering how much fun they were earlier in your life or thinking about new ones you might like to try. You will also find that many of these games have evolved to keep up with the times; for example, you might check out the Harley-Davidson, NASCAR, Golf or New York Yankees versions of Monopoly.

*Board games*: Backgammon, Balderdash, Battleship®, Bingo, Boggle®, Checkers, Chess, Chinese Checkers, Clue, Cranium, Go, Mah Jong, Mindtrap®, Monopoly®, Ouija®, Pictionary®, Risk®, Scrabble®, Stratego™, Sorry®,Trivial Pursuit®.

*Card games*: Bridge, Cribbage, Euchre, Gin Rummy, Hearts, Solitaire, Spades.

*Lawn games*: Badminton, Bocce Ball, Bowls, Croquet, Horseshoes.

## GARAGE SALES

(See Decluttering for a holistic view.)

## GARDENING

Opportunities: intellectual, physical, social
(if all else fails, you can talk to your plants)

There are tens of thousands of book and web resources for gardening so we will not attempt any significant distillation of that information here. What we will do is briefly visit different types of gardens that might respond to varying interests and the exigencies of space, climate and time.

**Bonsai** – Bonsai, which translates as "planted in a container," originated in China where the focus was on growing the plants in the form of dragons or animals. As Zen Buddhism began to influence Japanese culture, interest took hold in growing the small plants as an art form that intertwined man, nature and spirituality in a harmonious fashion. When Japan finally opened its borders to the rest of the world in the nineteen century, interest in bonsai spread rapidly. Bonsai plants are not miniature or dwarf plants. They are normal plants whose branches and roots are cut and formed to the size and shape the gardener/artist desires. The plant, pot and soil are seen as a harmonious whole. Many types of plants can be used in bonsai: juniper, pine, azalea, maple, spruce, cedar, elm, fiscus, even giant sequoia. You will need a pot, access to necessary sunlight, appropriate climate (varies by plant), some minor tools, some education and time for caretaking.

## Resources for Getting Started

*The Complete Book of Bonsai*
Harry Tomlinson
Abbeville Press, 1991

*Bonsai Survival Manual*
Colin Lewis
Storey Publishing, 1996

www.bonsaisite.com

(See also Zen.)

**Cacti and succulents** — These are "juicy" plants in that they store water in their leaves like aloe plants, in their stems like cacti, in their roots or some combination thereof. They have evolved this ability because they generally live in harsh climates for plants like deserts, mountain regions or maybe your living room. They need light, porous soil and a pot (if you have them indoors), occasional water — definitely not too much or they drown — and repotting as they grow.

## Resources for Getting Started

*The Complete Book of Cacti and Succulents*
Terry Hewitt
DK Adult, 1997

www.floridaplants.com/inter_cacti.htm

**Carnivorous** — Do insects "bug" you? Sic a carnivore on them! Carnivorous plants consume insects and other small creatures (no, your gerbil doesn't need to worry) as a form of supplemental nutrition. While most plants get their nutrition through their roots (water and minerals) and their leaves (where they manufacture carbohydrates), carnivorous plants, which tend to grow in poor soils (acidic, peaty, boggy), use acids and enzymes to transform tasty insects into nutritive juices. They can live without insects, but they are not as happy.

The traps these plants use are either "passive" — using sticky goo or slippery slopes like the lobsterpot or flypaper, or "active' — using clam-shell-like leaves with a hair trigger or trap doors like the Venus fly trap or the bladderworts. They can be grown at home, and you don't even need a license.

## Resources for Getting Started

*Carnivorous Plants*
Adrian Slack
The MIT Press, 2000

*The Savage Garden*
Peter D'Amato
Ten Speed Press, 1998

www.home.paonline.com/mrmiller

**Container gardening** — Want to be a gardener but you don't have good soil?  Or perhaps you live in an apartment and have no soil at all.  Or perhaps physical challenges make it hard for you to get to a garden.  Or perhaps deer or rabbits try to enjoy your garden before you can.  Consider gardening in containers.

Containers can be boxes, pails, barrels, pots, baskets and the like that you put on your porch, patio, deck, balcony, windowsill or hang on the wall.  You can grow all sorts of vegetables — lettuce, beans, beets, carrots, peppers, onions, eggplants, for example — as well as flowers.

Your containers will need to provide good drainage and you will need a planting medium that is pest free and drains well but holds enough moisture to provide for the needs of your plants.  Container plants in particular require regular feeding and watering.

## Resources for Getting Started

*Container Gardening*
Paul Williams

DK Adult, 2004
www.containergardeningtips.com

**Flower gardening** – Flower petals developed their shapes and coloring to attract insects. They work well with humans also! Whether cultivated annuals and perennials or wildflowers almost everyone enjoys the simple beauty of a flower. You can grow them just about anywhere, in the ground, in containers or window boxes, indoors or out. An aside: if you ever have the opportunity to visit the Keukenhof Gardens near Amsterdam, The Netherlands, from late March to mid-May (late April is best), seize it! It is the world's largest flower garden – more than seven million flowers and over 1,000 varieties of tulips – and it is gorgeous.

## Resources for Getting Started

*Complete Guide to Flower Gardening*
Susan Roth
Better Homes and Gardens, 1995


www.flower-gardening-made-easy.com/index.html

**Herb gardening** – Herbs (generally plants that do not develop a woody tissue) have a long history of service to mankind – the ancient Chinese, Hindus, Druids, Egyptians and Romans all wrote about the cultivation and use of these plants. Herbs have many uses:

Flavoring

Fragrance

Nutrition

Decoration

Lubrication

Cosmetics

Pesticides

Medicines

You might consider establishing an outdoor herb garden, if space and circumstances permit, or perhaps growing some in pots or planters in your home. You might, for example, grow aloe for treating your skin or grow cooking herbs in your kitchen. Bear in mind that if you decide to pursue herb cultivation, growing certain herbs is illegal in some jurisdictions.

## Resources for Getting Started

*New Encyclopedia of Herbs and Their Uses*
Deni Brown
Dorling Kindersley, 2001

*Your Backyard Herb Garden*
Miranda Smith
Rodale Books, 1999

www.herbsociety.org

**Mushroom gardening** – You can grow popular mushrooms for eating – button, shiitake, oyster – at home. Mushrooms are basically fungi. The part we eat is the fruit of the mushroom organism most of which is underground and is called mycelia. Growing mushrooms at home can be done most easily with kits that provide a sterile growing medium, spores of the mushroom you wish to grow and instructions. It takes 2-3 weeks to begin to harvest mushrooms.

**Resources for Getting Started**

*Growing Gourmet and Medicinal Mushrooms*
Paul Stamats
Ten Speed Press, 2000

www.mushroominfo.com/index.html
www.fungi.com/kits/index.html

**Rock gardening** – For the uninitiated: rock gardening is not about growing rocks (not enough time for that).  Rather, rock gardening is about growing plants that go well with rocks thus creating a pleasing overall esthetic.  Rock gardens began in Great Britain with folks who tried to replicate alpine scenes.  You can begin with your rocky area and enhance it or start from scratch by bringing in your own rocks.  Not having any land is not a barrier – you can also do rock gardens inside or on decks or patios!

# Resources for Getting Started

*Rock Garden Design and Construction*
North American Rock Garden Society, Jane McGary ed.
Timber Press, 2003

www.nargs.org/gardening/rockgardening.html

**Traffic circles, medians, etc.** – Traffic circles, medians, intersection triangles can all be interesting places to garden and add beauty to your community.  You'll need permission of the appropriate governing body and they may have some restrictions on height and color in order to avoid issues with traffic; on the other hand, they may provide you with raw materials.

**Vegetable gardening** – Most gardens are nice to look at; with vegetable gardens you can have the nice looks and eat them too! Wouldn't it be great to step outside and snip a head of lettuce and pick a cucumber and some cherry tomatoes for your evening salad? You can do that. Even if you don't have room for an in-ground garden, you can still grow vegetables.

## Resources for Getting Started

> *The Vegetable Gardener's Bible*
> Edward Smith
> Storey Publishing LLC, 2000
>
> www.thegardenhelper.com/vegetables.html
>
> (See also Container Gardening.)

**Water gardening** – I will always remember the contrast of walking along the dusty, noisy, hot, humid, diesel-exhaust-filled streets of Marrakech and then stepping into the clean, green and serene coolness of Yves St. Laurent's water-filled Majorelle Gardens.

Water is essential to our lives. A water garden nourishes plants (and maybe fish), reflects the sky, presents gentle sounds and movement and provides a focal point that joins us with nature's wonder.

## Resources for Getting Started

> *The Master Book of the Water Garden*
> Phillip Swindells
> Bulfinch, 2002

www.watergarden.com (click on "pond info" for helpful articles)

**Master Gardener** — If you enjoy gardening and would also like to help your community, consider becoming a Master Gardener. Master Gardeners participate in extensive horticulture training programs, usually provided by a state college or university. Following completion of training, Master Gardener candidates provide a period of volunteer horticulture service to the school and/or the community.

## Resources for Getting Started

www.ahs.org/master_gardeners/index.htm (programs for your state)

www.ahs.org  (American Horticultural Society)

www.hortmag.com (*Horticultural Magazine* — excellent info)

# GENEALOGY

Opportunities: intellectual, social

Where did you come from? What are your "roots"? Who made you who you are today (or at least contributed to you gene-wise)?

These and many other interesting questions can be answered with a little (sometimes a bit more than a little) digging into your past through genealogical research.

The research itself can be fun (have you ever wanted to be a detective?) and your work product can be satisfying to you personally and valuable to other members of your family (interesting idea for a gift).

*Talk to your relatives.* Begin your family history research by finding out as much information as you can from living family members . . .

Names of ancestors, their spouses, and their siblings;

Dates of birth, marriage, death, and divorce;

Places (town, county, state or province, and country) where these people lived.

*Borrow books from your public library on genealogical research.* These will tell you what records are available, where they can be found, and describe the research process. This is an extremely important step in your journey to finding out about your family past.

## Resources for Getting Started

*Shaking Your Family Tree*
Ralph J. Crandall
Yankee Publishing, 1986

*Unpuzzling Your Past: A Basic Guide to Genealogy*
Emily A. Croom
Betterway Books, 1995

*The Researcher's Guide to American Genealogy*
Val D. Greenwood
Genealogical Publishing Co., 1990

*Evidence! Citation & Analysis for the Family Historian*
Elizabeth Shown Mills
Genealogical Publishing Co., 1997

*The Source: A Guidebook of American Genealogy*
Loretto D. Szucs and Sandra H. Luebking
Ancestry, 1997

*Join genealogical societies:* The National Genealogical Society, the state genealogical society in the state where you live and the state(s) where your ancestors lived, and the county genealogical society in the county where you live and the counties where your ancestors lived. Membership usually costs relatively little (fifteen to fifty dollars) but you get a lot in return. Most societies publish newsletters and other publications that will provide you with information about genealogical research in the area, often including transcripts of actual records. Search the web. Some resources are free; some may cost a bit of money if you want to do more than basic research.

## Resources for Getting Started

*The Genealogist's Address Book* (4th Edition)
(names and addresses of genealogical societies)
Elizabeth Petty Bentley
Baltimore Genealogical Publishing Company, 1999

www.ancestorhunt.com

www.ngsgenealogy.org

www.archives.gov/genealogy

*Participate in the Genographic Project:* If you want to go as far back in your family history as possible based on genetics, you might consider participating in the Genographic Project being sponsored by The National Geographic Society and others to trace mankind's movement around the globe using genetics

Current thinking among population geneticists is that we probably all come from a common ancestor in Africa. Using DNA markers, the study's scientists and technicians can determine how our ancestors migrated from one part of the world to another and what genetic groups we and our ancestors are part of.

You can participate by purchasing a participation kit from the Project (one hundred dollars plus shipping/handling and tax). You provide a (painless) swab of your cheek and about 8 weeks later you can access a report that provides information on your genetic history and the movement of your ancestors. You can learn more and order a participation kit below.

## Resources for Getting Started

www3.nationalgeographic.com/genographic/index.html (DNA kit may be ordered here)

(See also Family Tree.)

# GEOLOGY ————————————————————

Opportunities: intellectual, physical

You don't need to be a "rockhound" to wonder where the rocks in your backyard or in the park, the woods or along the river came from. What are they made of? How did they get there? How old are they? Why are they shaped as they are? Why is there such a variety (or lack thereof)?

Or when you visit another part of the country or of the world, do you look at the mountains, plains, islands or unusual rock formations like The Baths in the British Virgin Islands or The Burren in Ireland and ask the same questions?

You can get answers to (most) of these questions without becoming a geologist or needing to acquire a lot of specialized knowledge. Basic books on plate tectonics and rock identification will take you a long way toward answering many of the questions on your own. You may also be able to find books on the geology of where you live as well as places you might be able to visit. Type "geologic history of (your state)" in your computer browser and you'll probably come up with some interesting information. (The author's home state of Connecticut is a fascinating study of colliding and splitting landmasses – Connecticut was once attached to what is now Morocco in Africa. The state's terrain reflects magma flows, ancient mountain ranges, erosion and the build up of sedimentary rocks like the Connecticut brownstone used in buildings from New York to San Francisco. The rock hard record of this history is available for you to see and touch; if you run your hand along the brownstone fence surrounding the Thomas Flood Mansion on top of Nob Hill in San Francisco, you are touching the bed of a 200 million year old Connecticut river.)

## Resources for Getting Started

*Earth: An Intimate History*
Richard Fortey
Knopf, 2004

*Smithsonian Handbooks: Rocks & Minerals*
Chris Pellant
DK Adult, 2002
*A Field Manual for the Amateur Geologist*
Alan M. Cvancara
Jossey-Bass, 1995

www.tmsc.org/face_of_ct (Chapter 8 reviews the geologic history of Connecticut.)

## GOAL SETTING ─────────────────────────

Opportunities: intellectual, social, physical

As you learned during your working career, setting goals is important for making progress, and assuring that things get done in a timely way and in a quality fashion. This is just as true in retirement . . .

What do you want to accomplish with the rest of your life?

What do you want to build or create?

Where do you want to go?

What do you want to see?

What do you want to experience?

How can you give back for all you've received?

What do you want to learn?

What do you want to do for others?

Who do you want to spend time with? Doing what?

What can you do to improve your physical well being?

Do you need to do anything to get your spiritual house in order?

While all of us will have some financial, physical and perhaps other restraints around our answers to these questions, they are important to ask. The answers give us a sense of direction about how we can remain engaged and live our lives as fully as possible. Consider making two lists . . .

Things to accomplish before I die (sort of the ultimate deadline); and

Things to accomplish by _____ (12 or more months away).

These can become your long-term and short-term goals. As with goals set in the work environment, they can and should be modified based on changing circumstances and new insights.

You may want to share your lists with your spouse or significant other (they may have lists also). This can be helpful as a reality check and for managing expectations. Perhaps you want to have some joint goals. But it is also important that you have goals of your own for which you will hold yourself accountable.

At the end of your short-term goal period, assess how you did. Did you accomplish what you set out to do? (Pat on the back?) Did you add or drop goals? Is there anything you fell short on? Should anything be carried over into the next short-term goal period? What additional goals do you want to set? Are there any changes to your long-term goals?

As you go through this process, it may be helpful to make sure you are setting goals that will help you remain engaged intellectually, socially and physically. If you have been making notes on items of interest to you in these categories, you can use them as a resource.

## Resources for Getting Started

*Goal Setting*
Michael Dobson, Susan Dobson
AMACOM, 2008
www.mindtools.com/page6.html

# GOLD PANNING

Opportunities: social (if you do it with others), physical

It may only be a flash in the pan, but it can be fun looking. Gold has been found in most U.S. states, but most frequently in Alaska, the western states, the upper mid-west, the south (Louisiana to Florida) and in the Appalachian mountain area.

Gold shows up in streams as a result of erosion. It is likely to accumulate in certain spots due to its relatively heavy weight and resistance to corrosion. A gold pan (they used to be metal but plastic is more common today) is used to separate any gold that may be present from the gravel in which it may reside. The gold panner partially fills the pan with gravel and water and then swirls the pan to wash out dirt and clay. The larger stones are discarded and the remaining material is examined for gold pieces. These are removed with tweezers (unless you are fortunate enough to find a nugget) and placed in a storage container. If you are patient and lucky you may accumulate enough to buy lunch. If it doesn't "pan out," then at least you had a good time outdoors.

## Resources for Getting Started

*Recreational Gold Prospecting for Fun and Profit*
Gail Butler
GemGuides Book Co, 1998

www. pubs.usgs.gov/gip/prospect2/prospectgip.html

# GOLF

Opportunities: intellectual, social, physical

When I first began thinking about retirement (beyond the financial preparation for it) I asked lots of folks what they were looking forward to doing. The most frequent response was "golf." Not being much of a golfer myself (I once won the prize — a golf doll whose head and limbs were joined with Velcro and designed to be ripped apart in frustration — for overall worst golf score at a gathering of insurance company executives) I thought: There has to be so much more. That, among other things, was an impetus for this book.

Yes, there is a lot more than golf, but golfing is good.

*Intellectually*: Your mind needs to instruct your body in the intricacies of the golf swing and the putt and then back off and not get in the way. You need to figure out which club to use, how much force to apply, which trajectory and line you want and how to achieve it.

*Socially*: While you swing the club yourself, golf is a social game. It is a great way to meet new people, impress them with your knowledge of the game's etiquette as well as your ability not to become angry with your ball, a wayward club or the course designer. Golf is also a good sport for mixed couples, since it relies more on concentration, strategy and finesse than muscle.

*Physically*: Walking a golf course is good exercise; riding a course in a cart is not as good, but at least you get to walk from the cart to the ball and back. You also get to enjoy pleasant, sometimes beautiful scenery and your exposure to the sun will assist with vitamin D creation and, assuming sufficient calcium intake, strengthen your bones (try asking your physician for a golf prescription). One note of caution. The golf swing uses parts of your body from your neck to your feet; done improperly (and sometimes even properly), there are a variety of ways you can injure yourself. An occasional lesson can assist with injury avoidance.

Many golf club, book and Internet resources are available and can be helpful.

## Resources for Getting Started

> *How I Play Golf*
> Tiger Woods
> Warner Books, 2001

(One of the best books I've read on golf.)

## GOVERNMENT ───────────────────────

Opportunities: intellectual, social

"Government is like a baby. An alimentary canal with a big appetite at one end and no sense of responsibility at the other."

—Ronald Reagan

President Reagan was talking about BIG governments in which those who govern are frequently out of touch with the governed except through polling. It doesn't need to be that way, at least on the local level where there is much greater chance to be heard and involved.

For instance, you can communicate with your representatives in government about issues that matter to you. You can find out who they are through your government's web site or by calling the government's offices. There are many ways to communicate but letter writing is one of the best at getting attention. E-mail can go missing and is easily deleted; phone calls may be noted but then forgotten. To increase the chance of your letter getting acted on, consider sending a copy to your local newspaper and/or the other members of the governing body on which your representative sits.

Organize others whose views are similar to yours to assist in supporting the issues.

Be persistent. Government usually moves slowly (and that can be a good thing) but it usually needs continual prodding to make sure it is in fact moving.

Get involved. If things aren't progressing the way you like, if government is becoming too much like Ronald Reagan's baby, you may choose to run for office yourself (and then you get to receive the letters). Or you might consider serving on some local government boards, task forces or commissions, such as Planning, Fire Services, Safety Services, Water Department Board, Board of Education, Zoning Committee, Public Works Committees.

These may be elective or appointive positions, but if you have the interest and time to serve, it is worthwhile making that known.

## Resources for Getting Started

*Moving Mountains and Molehills: Local Politics 101*
Al Arnold
SurgeBook Publishing, 2005

*Mobilizing the Community*
Robert Fisher, Joe Kling
SAGE Publications, 1993

www.statelocalgov.net (extensive links to state and local governments)

# GUN COLLECTING

Opportunities: intellectual

Gunpowder was invented by the Chinese in the thirteenth century. It did not take long to develop rudimentary cannons, then hand-held cannons, and eventually pistols, rifles, revolvers and automatic weapons. The history of firearms is intertwined with the last 800 years of human activity. Whatever your views of firearms, learning about their history and development can be interesting from many perspectives – technological advancement, historical impact, hunting, military or law enforcement activities, role in crimes and duels.

You might even want to collect fire arms for their beauty, workmanship, functionality or one of the perspectives referenced in the preceding sentence. You can also collect them as an investment – but as with all other investments, it pays to do your research. Brief story: my father, who was in the U.S. Army in WWII, expropriated two firearms – a heavily engraved double-barreled shotgun and an antique weapon with a funnel-shaped barrel – from one of Benito Mussolini's abodes. During tight financial times for his family in the mid-1950's he sold them to a gun dealer for fifteen dollars. One party to the transaction had done his research; the other had not.

If you decide to collect, be sure to check your local requirements for gun locks and licensing.

## Resources for Getting Started

*Flayderman's Guide to Antique American Firearms and Their Values*
Norm Flayderman
Krause Publications, 2001
(focus on antiques with information on gun collecting)
*The Collecting of Guns*
James Serven
Bonanza, 1964
(might be available in your library or second hand)

www.inventors.about.com/library/inventors/blgun.htm

www.nra.nationalfirearms.museum/collector/default.asp

www.armscollectors.com

# GUN CONTROL

Opportunities: intellectual, social

In contrast to the prior section, you may be more interested in controlling the ownership of firearms.

The oldest record of gun control the author could find was that of the Wampanoag Indian tribe in Massachusetts who signed a treaty in 1691 which required them to surrender their "English Arms."

Of course, attempts at arms control in general have been around far longer. The Old Testament talks about the need to beat swords into ploughshares; the second Lateran Council in 1139 prohibited the use of crossbows (but only against Christians); in 1588 the Shogun Hideyoshi disarmed the masses during what came to be known as "the Great Sword Hunt."

And there have been numerous examples of governments throughout history that have imposed arms/gun control to strengthen the grip of the ruler(s) and minimize the possibility of insurrection. From those examples comes the argument for the right to bear arms.

But almost all rights have some limitations. With respect to guns, consider . . .

*Registration*: should guns and gun owners be required to be registered?

*Eligibility*: Are there limits on who should be eligible for gun ownership? Consider age, safety training, mental competence, criminal record.

*Background checks*: should they be required?

*Waiting period to purchase*: should one be required?

*Carrying concealed weapons*: should this be allowed?

*Safety*: should there be rules regarding storage and locks?

Reasonable people can come to different conclusions on these topics, but if any are important to you, consider becoming involved in the discussion and actions as needed.

## Resources for Getting Started

*The Gun Control Debate: You Decide*
Lee Nisbet
Prometheus Books, 2001

www.bradycampaign.org

www.cato.org/pubs/pas/pa109.html

www.nraila.org/GunLaws/Default.aspx

# HABITAT FOR HUMANITY———————

Opportunities: intellectual, social, physical

This nonprofit, nondenominational organization provides houses for people who lack adequate shelter. Volunteers build the houses, which are sold at no profit to folks in need who are able to acquire them with a no interest mortgage.

Between 1976 and 2005, more than 1,000,000 people worldwide obtained housing provided by HFH.

While HFH loves to get volunteers from the building trades, you can get involved in the actual construction even if you lack any experience in construction. And if you'd prefer not pick up a hammer or paint brush, there are many other volunteer opportunities available.

## Resources for Getting Started

www.habitat.org (click on "Get Involved")

# HAM RADIO

Opportunities: intellectual, social

Ham radio is two-way radio communication between you (if you are interested) and people all over the world. "Hams" have their own radio equipment, which they can use to send messages across town or around the world by bouncing signals off the atmosphere or using satellites.

Why are they called "hams"? It was originally a term of some frustration used by commercial radio operators to refer to amateur operators whose signals got in the way of the commercial signals. Amateurs now wear the name with pride.

Most amateurs use the medium for fun and conversation. However, it can also be a very helpful public service in time of emergency when other forms of communication (phones, Internet, etc.) are not available.

You need a license to be a ham but the basic license requires only a 35-question multiple-choice test. Many children pass this test with ease (read: you can do it). If you want to upgrade to worldwide communication, you'll need to pass another 35-question test on slightly more difficult subjects.

## Resources for Getting Started

*Hello World: A Life in Ham Radio*
Danny Gregory, Paul Sahre
Princeton Architectural Press, 2003

*Now You're Talking: All You Need to Get Your Ham Radio Technician's License*
Larry Wolfgang
American Radio Relay League, 1997

www.arrl.org (web site of the national association for Amateur Radio – the American Radio Relay League)

# HANDWRITING ANALYSIS ─────────────

Opportunities: intellectual

There are two types of handwriting analysis: forensic (who wrote a particular document?) and graphological (what are the personality traits and characteristics of the person doing the writing?). The former is usually used in legal or historical settings to validate documents or signatures. The latter tends to be used in personnel selection or personal analysis. You can learn to do either or both, for intellectual stimulation or profit.

## Resources for Getting Started

*Handwriting Analysis: Putting It to Work for You*
Andrea McNichol
McGraw-Hill, 1994

www.handwriting.org

www.igas.com (International Graphoanalysis Society)

# HIKING

Opportunities: social, physical

Hiking can be great for mind, spirit and body. You can do it in small chunks of an hour or two, take a few months and hike an entire trail (like the 2,174 mile Appalachian Trail that runs from Maine to Georgia) or anything in between. For the short trips all you need is a good pair of hiking shoes and appropriate clothing; for longer trips, your equipment will vary with the itinerary.

Here are some famous options, where one can hike all the way or just for a day . . .

Appalachian Trail

Rim to Rim in the Grand Canyon

Ice Age Trail in Wisconsin

Oregon Coast Trail

Continental Divide Trail

American Discovery Trail: 6,800 miles, 15 states, Delaware to California.

Cinque Terra Trail: five towns in northwest Italy joined by a trail that takes you through olive gardens and vineyards. You get beautiful views of the mountains and shoreline; you can stop in the towns for lunch to fortify yourself for the next leg; train service will whisk you back to your hotel for a well-deserved rest.

Many hikers begin at home, doing simple trails that were former railroads, now converted to hiking and biking trails.

Or perhaps you'd like to climb a mountain (suggestion: start small). There are hills/mountains large and small to climb. From Florida's Britton Hill at 345 feet (not too tough!) to Alaska's Mount McKinley (you need to mount an expedition and get a reservation), each state has its own high peak. Perhaps you'd like to climb the highest peaks in your state, or perhaps a number of the highest peaks in various states.

You might try the sport of orienteering, for which you navigate through the woods using a map and a compass. You indicate a hiking route and identify turns in the trail. You can help assure hikers they are on the correct trail, as well as reduce trail erosion. Offer your services to the organization that oversees trail management.

## Resources for Getting Started

*Trailside Guide*
Karen Berger
W. W. Norton, 2003

*Orienteering*
Steve Boga
Stackpole Books, 1997

*The Appalachian Trail: How To Prepare For & Hike It*
Updated and Revised 4th Edition
Jan D. Curran
Rainbow Books, Inc., 2002

www.traildatabase.org (database of hiking trails around the world)

www.railtrails.org

www.americasroof.com/highest (highest peaks in various states)

# HISTORY

Opportunities: intellectual, perhaps social

Consider becoming an historian – a student of history. Since that is a very big topic, you would probably want to narrow your scope to an area of particular interest to you . . .

> Your town, county, state
>
> Your ethnic group or a different one
>
> Your religion, a different one or religion in general
>
> U.S. Civil War – lots to learn and places to visit
>
> Roman civilization (then visit Italy!)
>
> The tribes of Africa
>
> North American railroads (then go on a trip!)
>
> Perfumes
>
> Medieval times (knights, ladies, chivalry and so on)
>
> Political parties in the U.S.
>
> Your favorite sport
>
> Your favorite pet
>
> Your profession

If you develop sufficient expertise and perspective, you might then want to consider writing about what you have learned so that others can benefit from your insight.

## Resources for Getting Started

*The Landscape of History*
John Lewis Gaddis
Oxford University Press, 2002

www.wikihow.com/become-a-historian

(See also Writing.)

# HOOKED RUGS ————————————————

Opportunities: physical

Hooked rugs are made by using a small hook to pull strips of fabric or yarn through a backing medium like burlap.

In traditional rug hooking, strips of material are used to form loop piles above the backing material. In latch hooking, pre-cut strips of yarn are knotted around the backing material by means of a hook with a small latch; this forms an open knotted pile.

Both forms – traditional and latch hooking – can be used to produce rugs and wall hangings that are decorative and/or functional. Kits are available to help make your first effort a successful one (they worked for the author!). Hooked rugs make nice gifts since they are attractive in their own right and demonstrate caring due to the effort required to produce them. It is not hard work but it does take some time. You can certainly hook and chat or watch the tube simultaneously.

## Resources for Getting Started

*Rug Hooking for the First Time*
Donna Lovelady
Sterling/Chapelle, 2003

*Basic Rug Hooking*
Hooking Rug Magazine
Stackpole, 2003

www.rughookersnetwork.com

(See also Braided Rug Making.)

## INSECTS

Opportunities: intellectual

Insects are key to our daily lives. Among their fundamental tasks . . .

*Soil building*: they chew up and process into nutrients as much as half of all vegetation. This helps new plants to grow and keeps humans from being overrun by live plants and dead vegetation.

*Rendering*: they perform a similar service to the above with respect to dead animals, consuming more material than all the earth's large meat-eaters (other than humans) put together.

*Pollination*: they move billions of pounds of pollen in support of food trees and plants as well as the flowers that brighten our world.

*Making silk.*

*Making honey.*

*Making wax.*

*Making shellac.*

Of course, insects can also be real "pests." They compete with us for food, damage plants and trees we cultivate for visual effect, occasionally sting or bite us and can pass on disease. Clearly, insects are a mixed blessing. But we can't live without them, so we need to do our best to live with them. If that is the case, then it behooves us learn about them. And they are cool little dudes . . .

They predate the dinosaurs.

There are million of insect species, most of them not yet described.

Their skeletons are on the outside of the bodies, rather than inside like ours.

They exist in many environments from deserts to ice caves.

Many can function as teams.

They can be very fast in flight or on the ground.

Many have highly developed sensor systems.

Some of them engage in chemical warfare.

Some (like the ladybug) make their own antifreeze.

And, on average, there are somewhere on the order of 14 billion insects per square mile – there are definitely a fair number in your neighborhood. But this makes them easier to find and study. (Let's leave out the spiders. Spiders aren't insects; they're arachnids – more closely related to shrimp, crabs and scorpions than insects. You can study them too, but when you do, you're not studying insects.)

## Resources for Getting Started

*Alien Empire*
Christopher O'Toole
BBC Books, 1995

*Borror and DeLong's Introduction to the Study of Insects*
Norman F. Johnson, Charles A. Triplehorn
Brooks Cole, 2004

*A Field Guide to Insects*
Roger Peterson, Ed.
Houghton Mifflin, 1998

www.insects.org

www.colostate.edu/Depts/Entomology/links.html

www.xerces.org

# JEWELRY

Opportunities: intellectual, physical, social (beading party?)

Yes, jewelry can be fun to wear, but we are talking about *making* jewelry.

Beadwork for necklaces and bracelets can be an interesting and a simple place to start. Beads, string materials and clasps can be purchased in craft stores or on the web. You can create your own designs for your own use or as gifts. Beadwork can also be used to produce decorative items such as beaded balls, key chains, boxes, bottles, holiday ornaments.

You might then progress to stringing other materials – shells, enameled metal, artificial flowers, religious emblems, clay pieces, stained glass, wine bottle corks – with or without beads. The only limit is your imagination.

If your interest continues you might begin to collect bits and pieces of materials from broken or used jewelry such as clasps, pins, ear fittings and broach backs to use as components. With a few simple tools – needle-nose pliers, wire cutters, clamps, tweezers – you can begin to create a wide variety of pieces. You might even decide to begin working with soft metals.

## Resources for Getting Started

*Getting Started Stringing Beads*
Jean Campbell
Interweave Press, 2005

*Jewelry Making and Beading for Dummies*
Heather Dismore, Tammy Powley
For Dummies, 2004

www.geocities.com/SoHo/9555/beading.htm

www.jewelrymaking.about.com

(See also Wire Craft.)

# JIGSAW PUZZLES

Opportunities: intellectual, social

John Spilsbury, an English mapmaker and engraver, created the first jigsaw puzzle in the 1760s as an aid for teaching geography. He put one of his maps on a piece of wood, cut around the edges of the countries portrayed, and the jigsaw puzzle was born.

In its early years the jigsaw puzzle remained mostly an educational tool. But by the 1800's it also began to be used for entertainment (assembling pictures). Eventually, with the advent of power tools, the pieces became interlocking and some puzzles even became three-dimensional.

There are the cardboard variety with which we are all familiar (and which we probably have in our closets); wooden ones (Stave's, referenced below, will give you some options); virtual puzzles (see the online jigsaw sites referenced below).

What might you do with jigsaw puzzles?

*Solve them.*
*Collect them.*
*Make them.* (Can you use a "jig" saw?)

*Have them made from photos.*

## Resources for Getting Started

*The Jigsaw Puzzle: Piecing Together a History*
Anne D. Williams
Berkley Hardcover, 2004

*Making Wooden Jigsaw Puzzles*
Evan J, Kern
Stackpole Books, 1996

www.stave.com (wooden puzzles)

www.jigzone.com (online puzzling)

www.jigsawland.com (online puzzling)

www.jigsawpuzzle.com (make puzzles from your photos)

—————————————————————— **JOURNAL**

Opportunities: intellectual

So, why keep a journal/diary? There are many reasons . . .

Document and examine your thoughts and feelings;

Learn about yourself;

Reflect on events;

Record your history;

Find solutions to problems;

Work out your frustrations;

Comment on other people in complete privacy;

List your aspirations;

Make plans;

Doodle;

Watch yourself grow over time;

Develop spiritual insights;

Record your day/night dreams.

It's your book; you can put in anything you want. You can write it with you in mind as the only reader or with others as possible readers. If you want to keep things really secret, you can devise your own code system to disguise identities, places, etc.

You might also keep journals that are specific to a particular topic such as a trip or trips, your job, spiritual exploration, gardening, your pet, your health and so on.

## Resources for Getting Started

*Journal Keeping*
Carl J. Koch
Sorin, 2004

*The New Diary*
Tristine Rainer
Tarcher, 1979
(may be hard to find, but well worth it — check your library)

# JUGGLE

Opportunities: intellectual, physical, social

Yes, you can learn to juggle! You need a bit of persistence, focus and average eye-hand coordination. It is not much more challenging than learning to ride a bike.

Simple juggling kits, including things to juggle (usually small bean bags of some sort) and instructions, are available in game stores, some bookstores and through the Internet. Once you have mastered the basics, you can move on to juggling additional items or switch to other items like scarves, clubs, rings, balls, fruit or whatever. Do be careful with sharp objects.

## Resources for Getting Started

*Juggling from Start to Star*
Dave Finnigan, et al.
Human Kenetics Publishers, 2001

*Juggling for the Complete Klutz*
John Cassidy, et al.
Klutz, 1994

www.juggling.org

www.everwonder.com/david/juggle

# KARTING ———————————————————

Opportunities: social, physical

What comes to mind when I mention Mario Andretti, Emerson Fitttipaldi, Michael Schumacher? Formula One racing, right? Right!

What might not come to mind is Karting. All three champion drivers got their start in Karting. And while you may not have aspirations of being a Grand Prix driver, you might find Karting of interest from a variety of perspectives: kart preparation, competition or just the fun of driving a racing vehicle.

Age is no barrier to Karting, while there are lots of young folks involved, there are many older drivers who still enjoy the sport. And it can be fun to be around the young folks also.

There are basically two types of Karts:

> *Sprint Karts* — these are raced on relatively short (half mile or so) tracks. The races involve multiple laps and may be divided into different classes based on age and engine size; and

> *Enduro Karts* — these are longer carts that enable the driver to recline. They go faster than the Sprint karts and are generally raced on larger road racing courses like Daytona, Ontario and Mid-Ohio.

## Resources for Getting Started

> *Sprint Karting: A Complete Beginner's Guide*
> Jean L. Genibrel
> Motorbooks International, 2000

*Bob Bondurant on Race Kart Driving*
Bob Bondurant, Ross Bentley
Motorbooks International, 2002

www.worldkarting.com

www.brendel.com/racing/karting_glossary.shtml

---

# KITES

Opportunities: intellectual, social, physical

Go fly a Kite. Really! And you can build one too.

Kite flying goes back at least 2,000 years and perhaps as long as 3,000. The Chinese may have been the inventors of kites although there is also evidence of their early use in the South Pacific islands.

The Chinese built them of materials like silk and bamboo and used them for celebrations, worship, banishing of evil spirits and warfare. Chinese General Huan Theng supposedly tied noisemakers onto a large number of kites that he then flew over his enemy's camp site at night and frightened them away. Other generals used large kites to raise lookouts and observers of enemy positions. South Pacific islanders also used them for worship and as an aid in fishing.

Marco Polo brought the kite concept to Europe after his visit to China. While much kite flying has since become recreational, kites continue to be used in Asia for religious and cultural purposes. They have also been put to some very practical uses.

Leonardo da Vinci determined that he could use a kite to carry a line across a river. That discovery was put too good use by 10-year-old Homan Walsh; in 1847 Walsh flew a kite across the Niagara Falls gorge. The string of his kite was used to bring increasingly larger strings, rope and, eventually a steel cable across and thereby enabled the construction of a bridge that spanned the gorge.

Benjamin Franklin used kites to study the atmosphere, pull him through the water while swimming and across the ice while skating.

A kite was used to take a camera aloft to photograph the damage caused by the San Francisco earthquake of 1906.

The Wright Brothers used kites to help them design their airplane.

Paul Garber developed kites for use in target practice during World War II.

Okay. Want to connect with kiting (the flying kind, not the check-writing kind)? You have available a huge number of pre-made kites available for your use. Or you can build kites.

You can enjoy kites on your own, with your grandkids, with your own kids, if you are an active middle-age type, or in competitions. (There are even "fighter kites" — with which you compete to be the last kite flying.)

## Resources for Getting Started

*The Magnificent Book of Kites: Explorations in Design, Construction, Enjoyment & Flight*
Maxwell Eden
Black Dog & Leventhal, 1998

*Kite Craft*
Lee Scott Newman, Jay Hartley Newman
Crown Publishers, 1978

www.coda.co.za/kites_and_kite_flying.home.html
www.gombergkites.com/howgen.html (Professor Kite)

www.aka.org.au/kites_in_the_classroom/history.htm (Kite History)

www.webtech.kennesaw.edu/jcheek3/kites.htm (Kites w/ lots of kite links)

www.grc.nasa.gov/WWW/K-12/airplane/kite1.html (Kites / NASA site)

# KNITTING

Opportunities: physical, social

Knitting is a lot like crocheting in that you can make sweaters, hats, socks, afghans, pillows, towels, pot holders, golf club covers, cell phone or I-Pod covers and the like. It is different in that you use two needles vs. one in crocheting, and the stitching is different.

## Resources for Getting Started

*Vogue Knitting: The Ultimate Knitting Book*
Editors of Vogue Knitting
Sixth & Spring Books, 2002

www.learntoknit.com/home.html (differences between knitting / crocheting explained)

www.tkga.com

www.wonderful-things.com/newknit.htm (graphics on how to knit)

www.knitting.about.com

(See also Crocheting.)

# KNOTS

Opportunities: intellectual, physical (manual dexterity)

Ever wish you could tie a knot that wouldn't slip? Or one that could?

Using the right knots can add to your enjoyment of camping, fishing, boating or simply tying up your recyclables. Hitches, loops and lashes can help you hang things or join them together. Knots, braids and sennits (strands of rope woven in complex patterns) can also be used for decorative purposes such as mats, hanging chains and turk's head body jewelry.

Learning about knots can be fun, functional and educational. You develop a skill useful to you and others. You build manual dexterity. You can make gifts. You can learn about the history of knots: why they were created and how they developed over time.

Learning about knots is also an inexpensive activity. All you need is some rope and some guidance.

## Resources for Getting Started

*The Handbook of Knots*
Des Pawson
DK Publishing, New York, 1998

*The Complete Book of Decorative Knots*
Geoffrey Budworth
The Octopus Publishing Group Limited, London, 1998

www.earlham.edu/~peters/knotlink.htm

www.2020site.org/knots

www.animatedknots.com

## LANGUAGE

Opportunities: intellectual, social

"A different language is a different vision of life."

—Federico Fellini

There are many reasons to learn a new language. Among them:

Broadening your cultural and intellectual horizons;

Improving your understanding of literature, film and music;

Building new friendships;.

Ordering food and beverages;.

Stimulating your brain and helping with conceptualization and flexible thinking;

Connecting with people and culture when you travel;

Reading road signs and maps in other countries; and

It's fun!

You can begin simply with a basic course to see if you like it. Many towns, schools and colleges offer introductory or conversational courses. There are also tape, CD and DVD programs as well as web sites (some of them free).

Which language to study is usually a function of how you plan to employ your new language skills, e.g., travel to another country, connect with relatives who speak the language, communicate with foreign language-speaking folks in your community (Spanish may be a good choice for many of us), read foreign literature in its original language, watch movies without the subtitles.

You might also be influenced by how challenging the learning experience will be. Languages such as Chinese, Arabic and Hindi are more challenging for most English-speaking folks than Spanish, Italian or French. The author chose Italian because he likes traveling in Italy and because of its use in the music, food and art worlds.

## Resources for Getting Started

www.bbc.co.uk/languages (free language lessons from the BBC)

www.vistawide.com/languages/language_courses.htm (listing of language education resources)

# LEATHERWORKING

Opportunities: intellectual, physical

Wouldn't it be cool to pull out your wallet and, in addition to it being filled to capacity with twenty dollar bills, it is also a leather wallet you made yourself? You can also make your own belt, purse, passport holder, book jackets, masks, and lots of other useful and decorative objects.

You can buy the tanned leather, hand tools, metal fittings and finishing materials and start from scratch, but you might want to consider starting with a kit from your local craft store or from one of the many sources on the web.

## Resources for Getting Started

*The Leatherworking Handbook*
Valerie Michael
Sterling Publishing, 1995

*Leather Tooling and Carving*
Chris Groneman
Dover Publications, 1974

www.pslac.org/table_index_rawhide.htm

## LEGISLATION

Opportunities: intellectual, social

"There ought to be a law . . . " or an ordinance or a regulation.

Maybe there can be. If you believe a new or amended federal, state, county, city or town law or regulation is in order, assemble your reasoning (define the problem and your proposed solution) and direct it to your representative in the appropriate governmental body. If you want to add populism to your logic, present your idea in the form of a petition signed by as many of your fellow citizens as you can muster up.

Politicians are always looking to get their names in the news. If you have a real problem and a reasonable solution, you may be able to get their attention. Failing that, you could try direct democracy: developing an initiative to be put to a vote of the citizenry. The ability to do this and method of doing it varies by jurisdiction, and you would need to conduct your own research on the requirements.

Issues you might consider: the use of cell phones while driving automobiles, noise, parking, litter, term limits, treatment of animals, animal poop, dogs on leashes, solicitation, bicycles on sidewalks, jet skis, smoking, property maintenance, eminent domain, out-of-balance budgets . . . you get the idea.

## Resources for Getting Started

*The American Legislative Process*
William Keefe, Morris Ogul
Prentice Hall, 2000

www.thomas.loc.gov/home/lawsmade.toc.html (outline of the legislative process)

www.iandrinstitute.org (site dealing with direct democracy)

# LETTER WRITING ————————————————

Opportunities: intellectual, social

When was the last time you sent or received a letter or note that wasn't simply a brief exchange of information, an expression of congratulations or sympathy, or a "thank-you" for a gift or service? Yes, many of us do lots of email and may "catch up" or "touch base" with each other by phone or text messaging, it is not quite the same as a letter is it? A letter has a more substantive, perhaps more reflective, quality to it.

Once a year or so, whether I deserve it or not, a former colleague takes fountain pen in hand and writes a two or three page, single spaced letter to *me* (not one of those mass mailing things that come with some holiday greetings) to bring me up to date on where he is and what he is doing, where he and his partner have been traveling, how he feels, what he is thinking about and what he is planning for the future. I enjoy writing back to him along similar lines. Although I haven't seen him in several years, I feel we are nearly as close as we were when we worked together.

You might consider writing to friends or former classmates, teachers, physicians, colleagues or neighbors you haven't seen in a while and let them know how you are getting on and inquire about them and their loved ones.

You might also consider becoming a pen pal to a person in another country. We leave international relations to our political class at our peril. We can all be ambassadors, when we travel or when we write.

Or you might consider writing to one of our service men or women doing duty overseas to thank them for their service and talk about things back home. In return, you might be interested in their perspective regarding their work and their place of service.

And if you have a strong interest in and opinions on current affairs you might direct letters expressing your views to newspaper or magazine editors or your elected officials.

## Resources for Getting Started

www.ipf.net.au (letter-writing – not Internet – international pen pals)

www.anysoldier.com (can connect you with a soldier pen pal)

# LIVING WILL

Opportunities: intellectual

A Living Will, sometimes also called an Advance Health Care Directive, is a document that gives information to health care providers and others about your wishes regarding treatment if you are in a coma or have become mentally incompetent and are not able to consult with them directly.

For example, if you sustain a severe head injury in an accident and are in a persistent vegetative state, do you wish to be kept alive with feeding and hydration tubes? Or if you are terminally ill or the quality of your physical life is poor, do you want to be kept alive as long as possible or would you prefer to be kept as comfortable as possible with no extraordinary measures being taken to prolong your life? A Living Will can document your wishes with respect to these types of situations or any others that are important to you.

You may also wish to create a Health Care Proxy, also known as a Durable Power of Attorney for Health Care, which designates someone you trust as your agent to make medical decisions that are in your best interests, as you have described them, in the event you are not able to make those decisions yourself.

You can create these documents yourself using model forms (which vary by state) available in most libraries or on the Internet. However, you may feel more comfortable having them prepared by an attorney.

## Resources for Getting Started

*Living Wills & Health Care Proxies*
Martin Shenkman, Patti Klein
Law Made Easy Press, 2004

www.mayoclinic.com/health/living-wills/HA00014 (detailed discussion of the forms)

www.hcdecisions.org (information and model forms)

# LONG-TERM CARE INSURANCE ——————

Opportunities: intellectual

This book does not provide financial advice or discuss the pros or cons of various financial options. There is mention of several financial items you may wish to consider. Long-term care insurance — as its name implies, an insurance product that helps with the cost of long-term care after a predetermined period — is one of them. If you are very rich or of very limited means, you probably don't need it; if you are in between, it may make sense for you

## Resources for Getting Started

*The Complete Idiot's Guide to Long Term Planning*
Marilee Driscoll
Alpha, 2002

www.longtermcarelink.net

www.longtermcareinsurance.org

# MAGIC

Opportunities: intellectual, social, physical

Does the spirit of Howard Thurston, Harry Blackstone, Houdini or Cardini reside someplace in your being? Do you enjoy playing with children? Showing off for the neighbors?

Magic has been with us since ancient times. It has had connections with astrology, numerology, chiromancy, religion, science, medicine, technology and entertainment. It has taken many forms, among the main ones: white magic, black magic and illusion.

White and black magic deal with using charms, spells, rites, incantations, crystals and the like to bring about particular results. White magic was/is generally directed at bringing about good results: rain for the crops, a healthy child, a productive hunt, success in love, cure for disease, etc. — sort of the good Druid or witchdoctor type of magic. Black magic was/is directed at producing evil. If you are interested in black magic, you are on your own; I'm not going there.

Illusion is the area of focus in this section. You learned how to ride a bike? Shuffle cards? Tie your tie? Can you walk and talk at the same time? You can become an illusionist; it is a skill where practice is fun.

There are hundreds of tricks you can learn to do with just simple props: decks of cards, dice, cups and a ball, coins, handkerchiefs, scarves, newspapers and string. But while there are hundreds of tricks you can learn, it is probably best to focus on just a few initially and to learn to do those really well. Once you have your routine down pat, the next time someone at a dull cocktail party asks, "What's new with you?"or your grandchild needs to be entertained, off you go.

To keep it "magical," most professional illusionists will suggest you not repeat your tricks in the same session and, most importantly, never reveal your secret techniques.

## Resources for Getting Started

*The Complete Illustrated Book of Close-up Magic*
Walter B. Gibson
Doubleday & Company, Garden City, New York, 1980

*The Great Book of Magic*
Wendy Rydell and George Gilbert
Harry N. Abrams, Inc. New York, 1976

www.conjuror.com

www.magicsam.com

# MARQUETRY

Opportunities: intellectual, physical

This is decoration — for furniture, boxes, or just as decoration — created from thin veneers of wood and/or other materials. The art form dates back to the Egyptians but has been used throughout history and around the world. You can begin simply with some wood veneers, a craft knife, cutting board, glue, tape, pencil and a straight edge. As your skill and interest develop, you can move onto more sophisticated tools and materials.

You can connect with thousands of years of human creativity, sharpen your skills and make something beautiful all at the same time.

## Resources for Getting Started

www.marquetry.org

www.marquetrysociety.ca

www.marquetry.co.uk/main/hub/hub.shtml

# MARTIAL ARTS

Opportunities: intellectual, social, physical

Savate kyudo pakua iaido wushu jodo escrima pentjak salat.

No, that is not a tenet of Eastern wisdom. It is actually a listing of various forms of martial arts. Forms with which you may be more familiar (or at least you may know the names) include: judo, karate, jujutsu, kung fu, taekwondo and kickboxing. There are many others and various hybrids.

People have been studying how to fight successfully since people have had disputes that could not be resolved through reasoned discussion. The Olympic competitions, medieval jousting, dueling, the Shaolin legend, various treatises on combat and many other examples throughout history, as well as yesterday's newspaper, all point to our predilection for combat. So, why might you want to join the fray?

Perhaps you are feeling aggressive and want to fight with someone. If that's the case, I suggest counseling or alternative dispute resolution services.

If, on the other hand, you are seeking skills in self-defense, improved personal health and fitness, social interaction, participation in an art form or have just always been a David Carridine, Chuck Norris, Jet Li or Jackie Chan wannabe, martial arts may be attractive to you.

While they are "martial" because they are founded in combat, many of the martial arts require no physical contact at all. And you can focus as much on strength, grace and flexibility as on the underlying skills of movement and reaction. Remember: the Karate Kid spent much time reflecting on "wax on; wax off" before things deteriorated into fisticuffs and bloody noses. Also, while you might not know it based on what we are force-fed by Hollywood, most of these programs do not have a moral or spiritual code to which you are expected to adhere.

Try your yellow pages for schools to check out or type "martial arts" and your town into your browser.

## Resources for Getting Started

*Martial Arts after 40*
Sang H. Kim
Turtle Press, 1999

*The Complete Martial Arts*
Paul Crompton
McGraw-Hill, 1989

*Ultimate Flexibility — A Complete Guide to Stretching for Martial Arts*
Sang H. Kim
Turtle Press, 2004

www.martialinfo.com

---

## MASKS

Opportunities:  intellectual, social

Masks have been put to many uses, e.g. worship of gods, spirits or ancestors; healing ceremonies; fertility rites; frightening opponents in battle; hiding one's true identity for purposes good or evil; initiation ceremonies; dramas of ancient Greece or the Commedia dell'Arte; trick or treating.

Consider making your own mask or masks. You can use it for one of the reasons described above or simply for the next rendition of Halloween, Mardi Gras or Carnivale. They can also be great fun — making and wearing — with the grandkids.

## Resources for Getting Started

*Maskmaking*
Carole Sivin
Sterling, 1986

www.allspecies.org/edu/maskmaking.htm

# MASSAGE ───────────────────────

Opportunities: intellectual, social, physical

While the first thought that comes to mind is to get one for oneself, the real point here is actually to learn how to *give* a massage (and who knows, maybe you'll get one in return). This can be as simple as a neck, shoulder or foot massage, or perhaps you might want to get into something more ambitious.

While licensed massage therapists undergo extensive training and must pass a certification examination, you can learn enough to add real value to someone close to you. If you really enjoy the work, you might even consider making it a for-profit activity.

## Resources for Getting Started

*Massage Therapy: Principles and Practices*
Susan G. Salvo
W. B. Saunders, 2003

*Massage Therapy Cards*
Fiona Harrold
Connections Book Publishing, 2005

www.101lifestyle.com/beauty/massage/massage.html

www.holistic-online.com/massage/mas_home.htm

# MEDITATION ───────────────────

Opportunities: intellectual, physical

It is said that meditation can do a lot for you: relieve stress and tension, lower blood pressure, improve concentration, increase self-knowledge, help you find a deeper sense of purpose and meaning in life.

All that, and it isn't all that hard to do.

One of the author's first experiences with meditation was in an Oriental religions class in college. The professor brought in someone from a local temple to assist the 100+ students in experiencing the meditative state. Here's what he had us do.

> Sit comfortably — straight posture, feet on the floor, hands in lap.
>
> Close our eyes.
>
> Relax our bodies — ease tension out of our faces, shoulders, hands, feet.
>
> Take regular breaths and focus on following the flow of air in and out of our lungs — don't let thoughts intrude.
>
> Breathe only through the nose and focus on the air moving in and out past the tips of our noses — again, not letting thoughts intrude.

That was it. We spent about 15 minutes on 1-4 and 10 minutes on 5. The most frequent comments afterwards: "I didn't realize I was in class" and "I lost touch with my body." If it did that for college students, think what it can do for you!

## Resources on Getting Started

*Meditation for Beginners* (book and CD)
Jack Kornfield
Sounds True, 2004

*Mediation for Dummies*
Stephan Bodian
IDG Books Worldwide, 1999

www.meditationspot.com

## MEMORY STRENGTHENING ─────────────

Opportunities: intellectual, physical, social

It is a fact: the older you get, the more there is to remember. (If you are 60, it is at least three times as much as a 20-year-old). To carry this heavy load, you need to work at it, and it is not that hard to do once you "set your mind to it."

As we age, research tells us it is normal for us to require more effort to learn new things, to multitask and to summon up names and vocabulary. Absent illness or injury, our memory of how to perform tasks and our general knowledge remain unimpaired. It also appears to be true that our ability to reason remains healthy and the wisdom gained from decades of experience certainly enables us to make better decisions than when all those raging hormones got in the way.

So, absent illness or injury, while our mental skills may slow some, there is no reason to fear "losing it," if we keep our minds engaged. What actions can we take to keep our memory functioning effectively? These include:

Review the section of this book on Brain Exercise and training.

Take good care of yourself physically. Don't smoke. Be moderate in your use of alcohol. Stay physically active — what's good for the heart is good for the brain.

Be organized. If you have a place for everything (like keys) and put things in their place, and they are easier to find.

Keep and use a calendar.

When you meet new people, repeat their names and try to find a way to associate their names with their faces or physiques.

If you are going to be visiting with a group of people you know, review their names and the last time you saw them before the visit.

If you can't remember something right away, relax (tension gets in the way), focus (no multitasking) and concentrate.

## Resources for Getting Started

*The Memory Bible*
Gary Small
Hyperion, 2003
*The Harvard Medical School Guide to Achieving Optimal Memory*
Aaron Nelson, Susan Gilbert
McGraw-Hill, 2005

www.sharpbrains.com

www.helpguide.org/life/improving_memory.htm (background info and tips)

# MEN'S ISSUES

Opportunities: intellectual

Men, perhaps you'd like to involve yourself in issues affecting men (and others). If so, here's some areas you might address:

Boys without fathers

Divorce

Domestic abuse

Fathers' rights

Health and safety

Lifestyle

Single fathers

Work and family

## Resources for Getting Started

www.helpself.com/directory/men.htm
www.cyberparent.com/men/

# MENTORING YOUNG PEOPLE ───────

Opportunities: intellectual, social

All of us need help to be successful in life. In whatever you have accomplished in life, you probably had, from time to time, someone who took an interest in your success and gave you advice or guidance.

You might consider providing guidance, based on your experience, to a young person trying to find their way in a sometimes confusing world. Yes, that is the job of parents and teachers, but parents and teachers don't always have the time or sometimes the ability to provide what a young person needs. As a mentor you would provide additional help to whatever is available to the child from home or the educational system.

What kind of help? You might help with goal setting; planning for achieving goals; problem solving for issues at home, school or in social situations; tutoring; or simply being an understanding adult who listens and provides guidance and positive reinforcement.

You can identify mentoring opportunities through community organizations, schools and religious institutions.

## Resources for Getting Started

*Stand By Me*
Jean Rhodes
Harvard University Press, 2004

*The Kindness of Strangers: Adult Mentors, Urban Youth and the New Volunteerism*
Mark Freedman
Josey-Bass Publishers, 1999

www.bbbsa.org (Big Brothers/Big Sisters site)

www.mentoring.org (info on mentoring opportunities by zip code)

# METRIC SYSTEM

Opportunities: intellectual

Quick question: what do the USA, Myanmar and Liberia have in common?

Answer: The British Imperial System of weights and measures.

While we continue with ounces (of the dry kind), pounds, tons, inches, feet, yards, acres, ounces (of the wet kind), pints, quarts and gallons, tablespoons, teaspoons, cups, fractional portions of all of them, volumetric versions of some and Fahrenheit temperatures, the rest of the world (excepting Myanmar and Liberia) has gone metric, including the British.

Why did they do that?

The metric system is simpler, easier and more logical: it uses fewer measures, e.g. meters for distance, grams for weight; it is scalable using standard prefixes across measures, e.g. "kilo" for 1,000, "milli" for 1,000[th]; it uses decimals, which are a lot easier to work with in making calculations than are fractions.

The US Congress legalized the metric system for use in the US in 1866. In 1988, Congress declared the metric system was the preferred system for use in the US. What is holding us up? In large measure, it is probably the inertia of the familiar. But the world has gone/is going metric. The US will need to go metric as well, if we wish to remain competitive. How can you help? Learn and use metric; remember, it is simpler and easier than the system we use now that has its roots in the Middle Ages.

## Resources for Getting Started

*Metric in Minutes*
Dennis Brownridge
Professional Publications, 1994

www.themetricsystem.info/howtolearn

www.metric4us.com

www.unc.edu/~rowlett/units

www.lamar.colostate.edu/~hillger

# MISSIONARY
# OR ACTIVIST FOR A CAUSE ————

Opportunities: intellectual, social

If you have strong beliefs in something, e.g. human rights, religion, renewable energy, the environment, world peace, democracy, you might consider being a missionary or advocate in support of those beliefs. You can be a missionary overseas or in your community, through your religious organization or on your own. You can be an advocate in public or without ever leaving your home, in collaboration with others or on your own.

I have not included any web references as resources because most of the ones I reviewed were more aggressive in their advocacy than I was comfortable with or were too narrowly focused to be generally illustrative. A couple of books (religiously oriented, but the lessons are broader) that might be helpful follow.

## Resources for Getting Started

*On Being a Missionary*
Thomas Hale
William Carey Library Publications, 2003

*When the Members are the Missionaries*
A. Wayne Schwab
Member Mission Press, 2002

# MODELING

Opportunities:  social

When we think of models, what comes to mind for many of us are the fashion models we see in print, or perhaps the runway models pouting their way through a showing of a designer's latest work. These models, male or female, in large measure tend to be young, thin, tall and beautiful.

There are, however, many models who look more like the rest of us — (*please enter whichever adjectives come to mind*).

Clothing models who are not so young and/or thin are also needed and will be in increased demand as the baby boomers begin to move past middle age. Commercial or product models who look like moms or grandmas, executives, doctors, plumbers, coaches, truck drivers, attorneys, pizza chefs, whatever, are in demand all the time. You might be able to be a model for a photographer who needs someone who looks like . . . you.

How do you find these opportunities? Well, you might be "discovered" while walking down Fifth Avenue in New York. But a more productive approach is probably to send a letter expressing your interest along with several photos to some modeling agencies.

### Resources for Getting Started

*How to Become a Successful Commercial Model*
Aaron Marcus
Marcus Institute of Commercial Modeling, 1997

www.modelingadvice.com (advice on modeling and how to become a model)

www.modelnetwork.com/theagencies/afinder.cfm (list of modeling agencies)

## MODEL BUILDING

Opportunities:  intellectual, physical

You might have built scale models of cars, planes or spacecraft as a child. Consider what you might build as an adult: architecture (your house, your workplace or something more famous), sailing ships, steam engines, landscapes, battlefields, trains, dollhouse . . . let your mind wander.

## Resources for Getting Started

*Building Architectural Models*
Guy and Patricia Demarco
Schiffer, 1999

www.answers.com/topic/scale-model

www.scalemodel.net

---

# MUSIC

Opportunities: intellectual, social, physical

"Music is the universal language of mankind."

—Henry Wadsworth Longfellow

Since you are reading this book, English is one of your languages. Mathematics is another one. If you are computer-savvy, perhaps you can communicate in a programming language. Perhaps you know sign language (if not, I am sure you know how to communicate with at least a few hand gestures). A variety of studies have shown that learning languages stimulates our brains and helps keep them active and healthy — there are new words/sounds to learn and patterns of using these words/sounds that stimulate the brain's need for new things and the ordering of those things in some sort of structure.

Music is also a language. It can communicate happiness or sadness, joy or foreboding, peace or agitation, silliness or seriousness, simplicity or grandeur and many other feelings on the continuums of those emotions. It can physically relax us, lower or raise our blood pressure, challenge us, surprise us, help us learn, put us to sleep and wake us up (if we remember to set the alarm).

If, as Longfellow asserts, music is our universal language, it is also one of our oldest – flutes made of animal bone have been dated to more than 50,000 years ago in Eastern Europe – and most fundamental; studies have shown that infants are attracted to pleasant music and turn away from dissonant sounds. Meanwhile, every human culture has had some form of musical expression.

Okay. Music is universal and fundamental. What to do?

**Theory** – don't skip this! Theory is good! Theory helps explain why music is universal and fundamental. Theory will help you understand and appreciate your music and why you are easily able to distinguish it from noise.

If you have ever tapped your feet in time with a piece of music or hummed or whistled a melody, you are working with music theory basics. It can be very rewarding to your enjoyment of music to understand the basics of music theory; if you then choose to move on to more involved aspects you can do so, but even if you don't move beyond the basics, learning about them is time well spent. What follows are the basics of theory.

*Tones* – tones are sounds that have a particular "pitch" – keys on a piano produce tones; the keys on the left side of a piano keyboard have a low pitch, those on the right side have a relatively higher pitch.

*Intervals* – these are the distances between tones of different pitches. Think of the first two tones (notes) from the song, "Somewhere Over the Rainbow," and you are thinking of a big interval. Think of the first two notes from the song, "I Left My Heart in San Francisco," and you are thinking of a relatively smaller interval.

*Scales* – these are a series of related notes in ascending or descending order. Think of "Do Re Mi Fa So La Ti Do" from the movie "Sound of Music" and you are thinking of a scale, a "major" scale as a matter of fact. Major scales tend to sound happy. "Minor" scales tend to sound sad. What makes them major or minor? The intervals between the notes of major and minor scales are different and produce a sensation that is either up/happy or down/sad.

*Note values* – some notes are short in duration, some are long. Think of the beginning of Beethoven's Fifth Symphony: da da da daaaaah. You have three short notes and one longer one.

*Beat* – this is what you are following when you tap your foot while listening to music.

*Tempo* – this is how fast the music is played.

*Melody* – this is a series of notes played in an attractive sequence to a certain beat/tempo.

*Chords* – three or more notes played together. Chords are used to provide harmonic structure to a song. For example, if you were to sing a melody, you might accompany yourself on the guitar by playing chords.

*Structure* – music usually has a structure. For example, a song might be structured to include an introduction, two verses, a chorus and an ending.

If you were able to follow all of the immediately preceding without much difficulty, learning the basics of music theory should be quite achievable. There is, of course, more detail to what I have outlined above, but fleshing it out is what makes it interesting. If you enjoy it, you could move on to chord progressions, different structures, harmony and counterpoint. However far you take it, be assured that increasing your musical knowledge will increase your musical enjoyment.

**Play Music.** (Resurrect your old instrument or start anew on your own or with others.)

There are many instruments so we won't name them here, but it may be helpful to list some of those that are easier to begin to learn. Check out:

> *Autoharp* (also called Chorded Zither) – push the chord buttons and strum

*Guitar* — try nylon strings, if you are just beginning

*Harmonica*

*Irish* (sometimes called Penny or Tin) *whistle*

*Kazoo* — if you can hum, you can play it

*Piano/electric keyboard* — also very helpful in learning music theory

*Recorder* (the kind you blow into)

*Tambourine*

## Sing Music

A cappella group

Barbershop quartet

Church choir

Karaoke

## Listen to Music

Learn what to listen for (music theory helps a lot here)

Revisit your old record, 8-track or audiotape collection

Subscribe to a public symphony or college music program

Attend high school performances

Grammar schools (can be a bit painful at times but you'll love the enthusiasm)

Jazz clubs

Musical theater

**Compose Music** (See also the Composing section earlier in the book.)

## Resources for Getting Started

*Music with the Brain in Mind*
Eric Jensen
Corwin Press, 2000

*The Complete Idiot's Guide to Music Theory*
Michael Miller
Alpha, 2002

*Edly's Music Theory for Practical People*
Ed Roseman
Musical Ed Ventures, 1999

www.musictheory.net

# NEEDLEPOINT

Opportunities: intellectual

Needlepoint is essentially art produced with canvas, yarn and needle. The art can be the type you hang on a wall (I have a couple of needlepoint owls in my office who stare at me all day long to make I sure I remain productive) or it can be put to use for things like golf club covers, dog collars, book covers, watch bands, guitar straps, ties, cell phone covers and the like.

The canvas has a loose weave through which the yarn can be sewn. The canvas may come with a design stamped or painted on it or you might create your own design. You can also obtain designs that are on charts so that you follow the design section by section. Kits are available that will provide you with everything you need to complete your work of art.

## Resources for Getting Started

*The Needlepoint Book* (Also known as "The Black Book")
Jo Ippolito Christensen
Fireside, 1999

www.needlepoint.org

www.stitching.com/npg
(See also Embroidery.)

# NEIGHBORHOOD WATCH

Opportunities: intellectual, social

Concerned about safety in your neighborhood? Consider joining or starting a Neighborhood Watch group.

Neighborhood Watch groups bring neighbors together, in collaboration with law enforcement officials, to decrease the likelihood of crimes being committed in or near their homes. While the main focus of Neighborhood Watch groups is usually preventing burglary (theft of property), it also helps prevent injuries that occur during the commission of such a crime. Neighborhood Watches can also help reduce or prevent vandalism or other illegal activities that diminish quality of life.

Pro-active Neighborhood Watch programs may include security inspections and advice on improved locks and lighting from law enforcement officials; neighborhood patrols; marking valuable items with identification numbers; assistance to children and the elderly; disseminating educational material from the National Crime Prevention Council, National Sheriff's Association or local authorities; posting of Neighborhood Watch signage.

## Resources for Getting Started

www.usaonwatch.org

www.ncpc.org

www.usaonwatch.org/resource/Neighborhood_Watch/ watchmanual.pdf

# NEWSPAPER COLUMN

### Opportunities: intellectual, social

Is there a subject in which you have a strong interest? Can you write interesting articles about that subject in clear, correct and concise language? If you answered, "Yes, yes," perhaps there is a newspaper column inside you waiting to be released.

Folks with interests in travel, food, astronomy, pets, gardening, cars, weather, health, word usage/grammar, humor, social relationships, and a variety of other subjects have started newspaper columns. You may not get rich (if you get paid at all) but you may also get to see your name in print and have the opportunity to pass along your knowledge, enthusiasm and perspective. You also will be surprised at how many new friends you make!

To begin, survey your local publications to see if anyone is already doing a column of the type in which you are interested. If the landscape looks promising, write a couple of potential columns. Prepare a letter to the managing editor of the publication explaining your interest and commenting why a column of the type you are proposing would be of interest to the publication's readers. Include your sample columns and a list of potential topics for future columns (to demonstrate that this is an interesting field with much to write about). Follow-up with the editor after an appropriate interval. If at first you don't succeed, try another publication.

## Resources for Getting Started

*You Can Write a Column*
Monica McCabe Cardoza
Writer's Digest Books, 2000

*Freelancing for Newspapers*
Sue Lick
Quill Driver, 2007

www.columnists.com

www.writersdigest.com

(See also Blogging.)

# PAPERCRAFTS / ORIGAMI ————————

Opportunities: intellectual, social, physical

Did you know that paper — like wood — has a "grain" or orientation of the fibers? Take a piece of paper of some substance (not tissue) and bend (do not fold) two ends toward each other; then try bending the other two ends toward each other. Whichever way offers the greater resistance is the one in which you are bending against the grain.

There are many different types of paper and many paper qualities — like grain — that can be used to advantage in craft and decorative work. There are also many simple tools and techniques and materials you can use to enhance the appearance of your paper.   Think: fabric, lace, ribbon, pressed flowers, stamps, stencils, paint and the like.

If you are more ambitious you might try embossing or gold or silver leafing.

Projects to consider:

> *Book covers* – You use these to protect your books, identify them as yours (to be returned when you lend them out), or as a type of wrapping paper when you give books as a gift.

> *Cards* – Make your own greeting cards for special occasions. The recipient will know there is exceptional feeling behind the card that is sent.

> *Gift boxes* – You can decorate existing boxes with paper or make your own boxes out of sufficiently stiff paper. Wouldn't it be nice to serve your dinner guests postprandial truffles in small paper boxes of your own design and manufacture?

> *Gift wrap* – Make a gift extra special by creating your own gift wrap for it. Or make a gift of your gift wrap (and in so doing validate regifting as a good thing).

> *Hand-made wallpaper* – For the truly ambitious or Martha Stewart.

> *Holiday decorations* – For trees, walls, tables, mantles, doors.

> *Lampshades* – Having difficulty finding just the right shade? Make your own.

> *Origami* – This is the Japanese art of folding squares of paper into representational shapes. The word itself comes from two Japanese words meaning "fold" and "paper." Strict origami requires the paper only be folded; there can be no cutting or gluing. The paper airplanes you made in grammar school could be considered rudimentary origami. Higher levels of the art form would include flowers, birds, animals, insects, trains, planes and automobiles.

*Paper* — If you are really, really, really ambitious you might try making your own paper. This can be done by making paper pulp (essentially taking paper you have in your house back a couple of steps in the manufacturing process), adding other fibers — onionskin, cotton, coconut husks — if you wish, and molding, pressing and drying. Martha Stewart will be proud of you.

*Pop-ups* — You have seen these in books and greeting cards — when you open a page or card, something "pops" up. These can make for an interesting surprise or pointed communication depending on what you have "pop up."

A variation on the pop-up is the "exploding" 3-D shape. Here you take a 3-D shape — box, pyramid, circle — and make a two dimensional shape that is internally joined by a rubber band in a way that when pressure on the shape is released, it "explodes" into its 3-D glory.

*Sculpture* — If carving marble or casting metals is more than you wish to undertake, you might try sculpting in cut paper, paper mâché or paper pulp. You can start your sculpture from scratch or make it over a mold.

*Tags* — Place tags, gift tags, bookmarks are all good ways to start "small."

## Resources for Getting Started

*The Encyclopedia of Origami and Papercraft Techniques*
Paul Jackson
Running Press, 1991

*Greeting Cards & Gift Wrap*
Priscilla Hauser
North Light Books, 1994

*Quick and Clever Handmade Cards*
Julie Hickey
David and Charles Publishers, 2004

www.creativepapercrafts.com

www.papercraftz.com

www.shades4fun.com/makeit.html  (ideas/supplies for making lamp shades)

## ———————————PART-TIME PAID EMPLOYMENT

Opportunities: intellectual, social, physical

Many "retired" people work part-time for pay.

Some folks would have us believe that anything worth doing is worth doing for money. Without arguing the point, if you need additional income, then money is your driver and you should seek out opportunities that maximize your income. And some folks will have money as their driver because they just . . . like making money!

If, on the other hand, something other than money — fun, socialization, learning, whatever — is your main driver, then your world of opportunities for part-time employment is probably much broader. And if you can get paid for it too (and you find that acceptable — as opposed to volunteering your time), that's great.

It may be easiest to obtain part-time employment in the type of work you performed prior to retirement, but it may also be that working in a different field may provide a more satisfying experience.

A discussion on finding part-time employment is worthy of a book of its own and in fact a number of them have been written. Most review the normal search techniques of networking, responding to ads, approaching target firms, talking with recruiters, using the Internet and so on.

## Resources for Getting Started

*What Color Is Your Parachute?*
Richard Nelson Bolles, Mark Bolles
Ten Speed Press, 1994

*Second Careers: New Ways to Work After 50*
Caroline Bird
Little Brown, 1992

# PERSONAL HISTORY ──────────

Opportunities: intellectual, social

"There was never yet an uninteresting life. Such a thing is an impossibility. Inside the dullest exterior there is a drama, a comedy and a tragedy."

—Mark Twain

Consider writing your life story.

There can be many reasons for doing this, among them, to put your life in perspective, to create a record for your children or other loved ones, to create ties to a photographic record, to record your participation in events during your lifetime, to document medical issues that might be of interest to later generations of your family, to chronicle lessons learned from your failures and successes, to reflect on your loves and passions, plus many others. If you think this a project you might want to undertake, you might begin by writing down your motivation(s).

Unlike a journal/diary that is written for you, a personal history is expressly being written for others. Maybe it is a limited audience; maybe you don't want it read until after your demise, but it is being written for others. So you need to ask yourself, "For whom am I writing this?" Your choice of audience(s) will help frame your writing.

How much do you want to cover? While your story could begin with your progenitors and proceed to the present day, you may want to limit your scope to some extent, at least initially. Consider jotting down a timeline of the major events in your life (birth, parents, education, military service, work, marriage, children, friends, health, housing, etc.) and reflect on whether you want to do a summary of the highlights, focus on particular events, cover the entire story or some other mix.

If writing seems like too much work, you might consider making an oral recording of your history on tape or digitally.

Another alternative might be to employ someone to interview you and write your story for you.

You might also consider assisting a friend or a relative with writing his or her own story. This could be a way to try out personal history writing before tackling your own; or, if you have already completed your own, working with someone else could provide you with a new, fun project. Consider assisting a parent in writing his or her story; this could also help you develop some additional perspective on your own.

## Resources for Getting Started

*Legacy: A Step-By-Step Guide to Writing Personal History*
Linda Spence
Swallow Press, 1997

*How to Write Your Own Life Story*
Lois Daniel
Chicago Review Press, 1997

*Turning Memories into Memoirs*
Denis Ledoux
Soleil Press, 1997

www.personalhistorians.org

www.therememberingsite.org

(See also Photograph Albums and Journal/Diary Writing.)

# PETS

Opportunities: intellectual, social, physical (depending on the pet)

Pets can provide companionship and fill the need to nurture others that is present in most of us.

Studies in both the United States and Great Britain have also shown that people who own pets have fewer medical issues and doctor visits than those who don't.

While dogs and cats are probably the species that come to mind at first for most people at the mention of the word "pet," there are many other options, e.g., hamsters, gerbils, rabbits, guinea pigs, rats (not the yucky kind), mice, birds, snakes, ferrets and fish. If you have the space (your own or boarding), you might consider a horse or other large mammal.

In addition to space, other considerations include how much interaction you want to have with the pet (dogs and cats can give you interaction in spades, but you won't get much from a fish); whether the pet is best left "confined" (fish in tanks, birds in cages) or given the run of your apartment or house; whether the pet can be left alone (dogs need daily attention, litter-trained cats can be on their own for a few days); the cost of care and feeding.

You don't even need to own a pet to enjoy them and get the benefits of interacting with them. You might consider volunteering at an animal shelter or providing pet sitting or walking services (and get paid for enjoying yourself).

If you decide on pet ownership, do a bit of research on the pet and think through the commitment you are making. Pets can give you a lot, but they are a responsibility as well. You want to be pleased to have that responsibility.

## Resources for Getting Started

*The ASPCA Guide to Pet Care*
David L. Carroll
Plume Books, 2001

*The Healing Power of Pets*
Marty Becker
Hyperion, 2002

www.aspca.org  (click on "Pet Care and Nutrition" for excellent information)

# PHOTOGRAPH ALBUMS (PHYSICAL OR DIGITAL) —————————

Opportunities: intellectual, social

Are all your photos neat and organized? Are they being well preserved? Do you have back-ups of your digital photos? Can you easily find the photos of your trips to Saratoga and Sarasota? Can you put together a slide show of a loved one over the years? If someone some years hence were to look at your photos without you, would they be able to date them (other than through clothing styles) and recognize the people and locales?

(Full disclosure: the author's answers to these questions are a clear "no way." While I have photos of some trips in albums using clear plastic pockets and acid-free paper, I also have thousands of 35 mm slides in metal tray boxes with "year taken" labels on the outside and some minor notes inside on the contents, several drawers and boxes full of envelopes of unlabeled photos from the last several decades, canisters of 8mm film from my youth, cassettes of 8mmm video from my children's school years, and five large boxes of albums and photos from my mother going back at least 80 years of friends, neighbors and relatives some of whom I recognize and most of whom I don't. And since I went all digital a few years back, all my photos are on my PC, but none of them are backed up. I hereby resolve . . . to do something about all that, just as soon as I finish this book! )

If, unlike the author, all of your photographic files are neat, organized, well preserved and backed up, you should probably move on to another topic. However, if you are more like the author, here's what you might do.

*35 mm slides*: These like low light, low heat, low humidity, and vertical storage in a quality slide mount. Take a look at a sampling of your mounts. If the cardboard of the mount is yellowing or separating you may want to remount the slide in new acid-free cardboard or plastic. While reviewing your slides, add what labeling information you think might be helpful for you in finding particular slides and to later generations in understanding what it is they are looking at.

35 mm slides are photographic film and will deteriorate over time. If some of your slides are particularly important, you may want to have prints made as back-up or turn them into digital images. There are service providers that will do the 35 mm to digital conversion for you, but the service is not inexpensive. The other alternative is to use a scanner and create your own digital files. A scanner that can do 6 slides at a time can be had for about one hundred dollars as this is written. Once you have the photos in your PC you can organize them, e-mail them or burn them to CDs as you wish. Gift ideas: sampling of holiday photos over the years, retrospectives of and for your children, vacation highlights.

*8 mm movie and video*: This is probably best done by the professionals (although some do it yourself approaches are coming to market). Type "converting 8 mm to digital" into your browser, and you'll find lots of options.

*Prints*: like 35 mm slides, photos like it dark, cool and dry. Place them in plastic sleeves and store them in photo albums or boxes that are acid-free and PH neutral. Provide as much labeling information as you deem appropriate and worth the effort − in addition to helping you remember, think of who else might someday be reading your labels. The one hundred dollar scanner mentioned above can also digitize your prints. Some photography stores are beginning to use high-speed document scanners, which can digitize a higher volume of photos at a fairly reasonable cost but at a lower resolution than you will get with your scanner.

*Digital photos on your PC*: Organizing your photos on your PC is usually simple, using software that came with your machine or with relatively low cost software you add on your own. Of utmost importance is backing up your photo files (all your files for that matter, but this is the section on photos so we'll stick with that). Burning a CD or CDs of your photos or copying your photo files to a back-up disk or other storage device is straightforward and well worth the time it takes to learn to do it.

You can also store photos at various storage, file sharing and photo services sites on the Internet for free or at low cost (they make their money in other ways, like selling you prints). Choose carefully if you take this route – if the site goes bust, where will your photos be?

Received photos: if you think you may be the recipient of a significant volume of family photos someday, you might encourage the current holders of those photos to provide a bit of written guidance as to who's who and what were the physical settings. It could save you a lot of chin scratching in the future.

## Resources for Getting Started

*Conservation of Photos*
George Eaton
Eastman Kodak, 1985

*An Ounce of Preservation: A Guide to the Care of Papers and Photographs*
Craig A. Tuttle
Rainbow Books, Inc., 1995

www.homemoviesday.com/preservation.html
www.geocities.com/heartland/6662/photopre.htm
www.loc.gov/preserve/care/photo.html

# PHOTOGRAPHY

(See Art.)

# PHYSICAL FITNESS

Opportunities: physical

Numerous studies have shown that regular physical activity can reduce the risks associated with high blood pressure, obesity, adult-onset diabetes, colon cancer and other diseases and conditions. Simply walking at a vigorous pace for 30 minutes five times per week can make a significant difference. As with any physical activity, just make sure you have your doctor's blessing before you begin.

If you are already with the program, hooray for you and keep up the good work. If you are not with the program, please reread the previous paragraph.

## Resources for Getting Started

AARP offers a free *Physical Activities Workbook* that can help you get started and keep you going. Call Toll Free 1-888-687-2277.

(See also Exercise, Walking and Weightlifting.)

# PHYSICAL EXAM

Opportunities: physical

Even if you feel great, physical exams are important to screen for diseases and physical changes you may not notice on your own, to assure your vaccinations are up to date, to get advice on healthy living and for maintaining a relationship with a physician in case you do become ill.

You cannot detect problems with blood pressure, blood sugar and cholesterol without having them checked.

Your physician will guide you on how often you should have tests and screenings, but you should have them. Hey, you bring your car in for service, why not your body?

## Resources for Getting Started

*Health Assessment & Physical Examination*
Mary Ellen Zater Estes
Centage Delmar Learning, 2006

www.drugs.com/enc/physical-exam-frequency.html
www.healthcare.org/tag/physical-exam-frequency

# PICNIC

Opportunities: intellectual (bring a book), social (bring a friend)

Are you doing the same old thing for lunch each day? Why not plan a picnic to a local park or garden? And since the original meaning of picnic was a meal at which everyone contributed something, why not do it with a friend or friends with whom you can share both food and the experience?

## Resources for Getting Started

Reach out to family members or call friends to join you.

# PHILOSOPHY

Opportunities: intellectual

Who am I?

Why am I here?

Why is there something instead of nothing?

What is the meaning of life?

What is happiness?

What is truth?

What is free will? Do I have it?

What is the difference between good and evil?

What happens when I die?

Where are we going? (And why are you carrying that hand basket?)

Perhaps you find the answers to these questions in religion. Perhaps you find them elsewhere. Perhaps you aren't sure or don't know.

Philosophers are seekers of wisdom and truth. To the extent you seek and begin to develop answers, you too are a philosopher.

## Resources for Getting Started

*The Story of Philosophy*
Will Durant
Pocket Books, 1991

*Philosophy: A Very Short Introduction*
Edward Craig
Oxford University Press, 2002

*Man's Search for Meaning*
Victor Frankel
Pocket Books, 1997

www.garlikov.com/Philosophy.html

(See also Zen.)

# PILGRIMAGE

Opportunities: intellectual

Is there a place to which you have not been but is nonetheless very special for you? It could be special for reasons religious or secular, but visiting it would be likely to strike a strong emotional chord. Maybe it is worth a trip.

> *Religious*: Jerusalem, Rome, Canterbury, Santiago de Compostela, Lourdes, Mecca, Mesada, Mount Athos, Wittenberg.

> *Family*: homes, immigration points, country/city of origin, burial places.

> *Secular*: seats of government, battlefields, wilderness sites, birthplaces or workplaces of people who changed the world for the better, great architecture, sites of great sacrifice, places where something of great significance began.

## Resources for Getting Started

www.york.ac.uk/projects/pilgrimage

# PHYSICAL AGING

Opportunities: intellectual, social, physical

If you are reading this book it is more than likely that you have attained at least the middle years of your life. The physical aging "process" takes place over many years beginning as early as our 20s according to some experts. It affects our hearing, our hair, our eyesight, our ability to smell and taste, our muscles, joints, skin, metabolism, digestive and "related" processes, memory, sexual activity and a number of other areas.

While the process is, at least at this point in time, inevitable, there are many actions we can take to slow it down and, in some cases, counteract parts of it. It behooves us then to do our best to understand the process and what we can do to ameliorate whatever we find unattractive about it.

Learn about the aging process. You are living it so why not try to understand it? Decide what, if anything, you want to do in response. The answer to that should probably be, "Develop and/or implement your action plan."

## Resources for Getting Started

*Living to 100: Lessons in Living to your Maximum Potential at any Age*
Thomas T. Perls, Margery Hutter Silver
Basic Books 1999

*How and Why We Age*
Leonard Hayflick
Ballantine Books 1994

*Successful Aging*
Robert Louis Kahn, John Wallis Rowe
Delacorte Press 1999

*Maximum Life Span*
Ray Walford
Simon and Schuster 1983

www.nia.nih.gov (National Institute on Aging)

www.aging.ucla.edu (University of California at Los Angeles Center on Aging)

www.infoaging.org (American Foundation for Aging Research)

www.hcoa.org (Huffington Center on Aging)

# POETRY

Opportunities: intellectual

At last, when all the summer shine
That warmed life's early hours is past,
Your loving fingers seek for mine
And hold them close—at last—at last!

—Elizabeth Akers Allen

Poetry has a special ability to capture or evoke an insight, a moment or a feeling as is evident from the first few lines of Elizabeth Akers Allen's poem "At Last". The word "poetry" derives from the ancient Greek *poieo* meaning, "I create." It was an oral art form before writing was invented. Because it uses words and their sounds to create images and feelings rather than just convey information, poetry is often difficult to translate into other languages. Indeed, Robert Frost said, "Poetry is the first thing lost in translation."

Ancient poems focused on oral history and liturgy. They had rhythm but did not rhyme. With the advent of the lyre, poems began to be sung; from this we get our modern day *lyric*. Arab poets were probably the first to use rhyming, and it was later adopted in Europe and elsewhere.

There are many forms of poetry. The forms vary based on the length of the work, rhythm, whether or not rhyming is employed and various other factors. Of course, any poetic "rule" can be bent or broken as the need calls for right up to and including "free" form. The most common forms:

*Ballad*: Think "Casey at the Bat," "Robin Hood"

*Couplet*:  A rhyming form based on a-a, b-b, c-c, e.g.

> *A little learning is a dangerous thing;* (a)
> *Drink deep, or taste not the Pierian spring.* (a)
> *There shallow draughts intoxicate the brain,* (b)
> *And drinking largely sobers us again.* (b)

> —Alexander Pope

*Epic*: Think Iliad, Odyssey, Beowulf

*Haiku*:  The Haiku is a short poetry form originating in Japan. The subject matter is frequently a moment in time and, in Japanese Haiku, frequently about something occurring in nature. As adopted in the Western world the form is generally three lines or less (with the second line being longer syllabically than the first and the third), uses seventeen syllables or less and can generally be spoken in one breath.

Since I've always wanted to publish a poem, here's my poem:

> Leaves fall on the water.
> A stream slowly flows away.
> Thoughts follow the leaves.
>
> —R. K. Price

*Limerick*: this form is short, usually funny and almost as frequently ribald. It uses five lines with an aabba rhyming scheme.

> There was a young lady from Niger
> Who smiled as she rode on a tiger.
> They returned from the ride
> With the lady inside,
> And the smile on the face of the tiger.
>
> —Anonymous

*Sonnet*: "Sonnet" is derived from the Italian word *sonetto* meaning "little song." It is generally 14 lines in length, uses three quartrains (four lines of verse) and follows the form *a-b-a-b, c-d-c-d, e-f-e-f, g-g* although lots of other variations are possible. Shakespeare did much to popularize the form (he wrote over 150 sonnets) and it has been used by such poetic greats as Donne, Wordsworth, Keats, Shelly, Browning, Yeats and Frost. Here is number 116 from the Bard:

> Let me not to the marriage of true minds
> Admit impediments. Love is not love
> Which alters when it alteration finds,
> Or bends with the remover to remove:
> O, no! it is an ever-fixed mark,

That looks on tempests and is never shaken;
It is the star to every wandering bark,
Whose worth's unknown, although his height be taken.
Love's not Time's fool, though rosy lips and cheeks
Within his bending sickle's compass come;
Love alters not with his brief hours and weeks,
But bears it out even to the edge of doom.
If this be error and upon me proved,
I never writ, nor no man ever loved.

If life became too busy for you to connect with poetry, now may be your opportunity. There is something for everyone. Poetry can be light, deep, short, long, passionate, happy, sad, lecherous, enlightening, whatever you might be seeking.

You can also write poetry yourself, perhaps starting with some short forms like the Haiku or something funny like the limerick. Issac Asimov, the prodigious writer of science fiction, found that writing limericks was so much fun and made so many people laugh that he produced several books of them.

## Resources for Getting Started

*In the Palm of Your Hand: The Poet's Portable Workshop*
Steve Kowit
Tilbury House Publishers, 1993

*The Poet's Companion*
Kim Addonizio, Dorianne Lauz
W.W. Norton & Co., 1997

www.poetrysociety.org (lots of help, tools, poems)

# POLITICS

Opportunities: intellectual, social

"If liberty and equality, as is thought by some, are chiefly to be found in democracy, they will be best attained when all persons alike share in the government to the utmost."

—Aristotle

"Democracy is the recurrent suspicion that more than half of the people are right more than half of the time."

—E. B. White

Just as a successful retirement depends on being engaged, so does success in politics and government. Our political system is based on the beliefs that if most of us don't like the way things are going, we can effect change and that, in the process, each of our voices and votes is important.

How do we do that?

Stay informed about current issues — read, listen, think, discuss. Communicate your views to your representatives.

Contribute your time and money as you can to those causes you believe in and the people you think can best represent your interests.

Vote and encourage others to do so also. In a democracy, if you don't vote you lose your right to complain.

If all else fails, consider running for office yourself.

A suggestion: do all of the above while being courteous to others and considerate of opposing viewpoints. The embarrassing national political imbroglio of recent years — name-calling, truth spun beyond all recognition, epithet-hurling, party above principle, interrupting and shouting down other speakers and the like — demeans our institutions. Be vigorous in espousing and defending your views. But the best outcome will probably result when all views are given fair hearing and consideration. In addition, that approach will probably result in the greatest measure of support for the outcome.

## Resources for Getting Started

*Politics for Dummies*
Ann DeLaney
For Dummies, 2002

*Running For Office*
Ronald Faucheux
M. Evans & Company, 2002

www.democrats.org (Democratic National Committee web site)

www.rnc.org (Republican National Committee web site)

(See also Congress and Government.)

# POTTERY

Opportunities: intellectual, physical

Seven thousand years ago, or thereabouts, one of our progenitors burned a cord and clay basket (probably used to hold seeds or grain) in a fire and discovered that fired clay becomes hard. Other progenitors in various parts of the world made similar discoveries and this led to wide-spread use of pots, bowls, dishes, religious figurines, decorative pieces and other items fashioned from clay.

Clay is found below the soil level in most parts of the world. In its pure form it is composed of silica and alumina particles (the smaller the better) and water; however, most clay contains a number of impurities, since it is typically covered with earth.

In addition to its characteristic hardening when fired, clay's other main quality is its plasticity or ability to hold its shape while being formed into a pot, dish or statue of your uncle Ed.

There are two main methods for hand-shaping clay for pottery:

> *Handwork* — forming balls, ropes, and slabs into the desired shape. This technique is usually used for objects other than round symmetrical ones.

> *Wheelwork* — placing a ball of clay onto an electric or foot driven wheel and forming the clay with your hands into the desired shape as the wheel turns. This method is used for round symmetrical objects like plates, bowls and vases.

Wheelwork can have handwork added after it has been formed, e.g. adding handles to a vase. Different additives can be mixed with the clay to provide color and texture.

After the clay dries it is "fired" — heated in an oven or kiln. This changes the clay into ceramic — a much stronger material. Clay that is fired at relatively low temperatures remains somewhat porous and is called "terra cotta" or "earthenware;" clay that is fired at higher temperatures and vitrifies (becomes glassy) is much stronger and is called "stoneware."

The pottery may then be coated with a decorative glazing (a material that will form a glass coating) and fired a second time.

Pottery can provide the satisfaction of making things and being part of an almost 10,000-year-old craft. It also can be a source of functional and decorative items as well as gifts, or perhaps items you might sell. A large number of suppliers of tools and materials can be found on the web by directing your search engine to "pottery sup-plies." You can usually also take classes through community education programs or perhaps at a potter's studio.

## Resources for Getting Started

*The Complete Potter's Companion*
Tony Birks
Bulfinch, 1998

*Thrown Pottery Techniques Revealed*
May Chappelhow
Krause, 2001

www.ceramicartsdaily.org

www.artshow.com/resources/ceramics.html

# PRISONERS

Opportunities: intellectual, social

There are over 2 million inmates of Federal and State prisons or local jails. This represents about 0.7 percent of the U.S. population, a higher percentage than any other nation.

The purposes of prisons are to protect society from criminals through incarceration, punish criminals for their offenses by taking away freedom, while preparing prisoners to reenter society through education and rehabilitation programs. While prisons perform some of theses tasks quite well, a recidivism rate of over 60 percent indicates room for improvement. What to do?

You might consider volunteering to visit with prisoners or to teach classes that assist with rehabilitation. If you don't wish to visit in person or there is no prison near you, you might consider becoming a pen pal of a prisoner. You could also become knowledgeable about prison-related issues and lobby your representatives for improvements.

## Resources for Getting Started

*Chicken Soup for the Prisoner's Soul*
Jack Canfield, Mark Hansen, Tom Lagana
HCI, 2002

*Behind Bars*
Jeffery Ross, Stephen Richards
Alpha, 2002

www.pfm.org (Prison ministry founded by Chuck Colson of Watergate fame)

www.going-straight.com/links.shtml (Links to a variety of prison-related sites)

# PUPPETEERING

Opportunities: social, physical

Do you feel there is an actor inside you but getting on stage gives you the jitters? Perhaps you'd like to try puppeteering.

Puppets were used in ancient China, Egypt, and Greece. The Christian Church used them for religious instruction during the Middle Ages. The children's show "Sesame Street" continues to use them today.

The are several types of puppets, e.g. "Kukla, Fran and Ollie" (hand puppets); "Howdy Doody" and "Phineas T. Bluster" (marionettes); "Jerry Mahoney" and "Charlie McCarthy" (ventriloquist dummies); and "The Muppets" (rod puppets).

Puppets can be used for academic or religious education, for entertainment of people of all ages and as an art form. They can also be interesting construction projects, perhaps in conjunction with construction of a theater. This could be something you do for or with children and perhaps put it to use in schools or nursing homes.

## Resources for Getting Started

*101 Hand Puppets: A Beginner's Guide to Puppeteering*
Richard Cummings
Dover Publications, 2002

*Puppets and Puppet Theatre*
David Currell
Crowood Press, 1999

www.sagecraft.com/puppetry

www.user.ultinet.net/~kfo

## QUIT SMOKING

Enough said.

## Resources for Getting Started

www.cdc.gov/tobacco/quit-smoking/index.htm
www.smokefree.gov

# RADIO

Opportunities: intellectual

The "long" and the "short" of it.

You are familiar with listening to AM and FM radio. You may also know CB (Citizen's Band used by the general public for two-way communication), UHF (used by boaters and others) and Satellite (Sirius and XM). Additional choices include LW (long wave) and SW (short wave), and these are the subjects of this section.

AM and FM radio transmissions are essentially local (although AM transmissions can travel farther after sunset when the AM signal can bounce off the ionosphere). SW and LW transmissions bring you the rest of the world: the BBC, Radio Moscow, Radio Havana, Radio Netherlands, Voice of Free China, Vatican City, Radio Australia, etc. Most countries have English language broadcasts, frequently directed at listeners in the United States, and it is interesting to get their slants on the news. Radio Havana, in particular, can be hilarious.

Of course, you can also get broadcasts in local languages and music from the local culture. This can be particularly interesting if you are planning to visit the country, are studying the language or are trying to connect with your roots. Beyond the large country-sponsored stations mentioned above, you can also tune into smaller commercial stations broadcasting from just about anywhere (if life is getting too tense, perhaps some happy music from the Caribbean would be in order).

As with CB, UHF and Satellite, you need a special receiver which can be had for as little as fifty dollars, but a somewhat larger investment will provide you with many more features and better reception.

## Resources for Getting Started

*Passport to Worldband Radio*
Lawrence Magne
International Broadcasting Services, 2008

www.ac6v.com/swl.htm (Lots of information and frequency listings)

www.support.radioshack.com/support_tutorials/communications/swave-0.htm (tutorial on short wave radio)

# READING

Opportunities: intellectual

"Reading is to the mind what exercise is to the body."

—Sir Richard Steele

Reading is one of the great joys of life. You get to see the world through another's person's eyes. You get to travel, meet new people, taste new foods, and learn about relationships, history, art, politics and myriad other subjects. In the world of fiction, you get to escape for a bit from your daily existence and step into someone else's existence. All this without leaving your easy chair.

Okay, you say. Reading is good. What to do?

Join or form a book club so you can share the joy of reading with others. See the section on Book Clubs.

Reread your favorites from your youth. (Do you have any different insights or feelings?)

Read everything by one author and become an expert!

Become an expert in a particular genre.

Tackle one or more of the "best 100" lists. (See also Resources.)

Consider balancing fiction and non-fiction and minimizing the trashy stuff. As John Ruskin put it, "Life being very short, and the quiet hours of it few, we ought to waste none of them in reading valueless books."

## Resources for Getting Started

www.ilovelibraries.org/booklovers/index.cfm
www.randomhouse.com/modernlibrary/100best.html
www.ala.org/recommendedreading (American Library Association)
http://www.nypl.org/branch/books/booklists.cfm (booklists from the New York Public Library)
www.literarycritic.com/adler.htm (for the truly ambitious, Mortimer Adler's list to the 100 Great Books)

Your nearest library or bookstore.

# RECIPES

Opportunities: intellectual, social

Are they taking over your kitchen shelves, closets and drawers? Is it time to get them organized? Some options:

Toss or donate cookbooks you don't use.

Keep the recipe, not the magazine.

Group the recipes you want to keep into categories that make sense to you and then put them into your choice of one of the following:

Three-ring binders;

Photo albums;

Colored file folder with pockets;

File box with hanging folders;

A-Z accordion file;

Shoebox with file cards;

Scanner/computer (remember to do back-ups).

Perhaps your religious institution or social group might be interested in obtaining everyone's favorite recipes to put into a book for use by all.

You might also consider gathering you children's favorite recipes into a book as a present for them when they move into their own abodes.

## Resources for Getting Started

www.recipecentersoftware.com (free recipes and recipe management software)
www.ehow.com/how_134792_organize-recipes-cookbooks.html

## RELIGION

Opportunities: intellectual, social

Pop quiz time. Identify the religion that has the following tenets:

Belief in one God;

Belief in God's angels;

Belief in God's prophets or messengers, such as those of the

Hebrew Bible, John the Baptist and Jesus;

Belief in sacred texts, such as the New Testament and the Torah;

Belief that God is the creator and sustainer of the universe and that, while God is all-knowing and all-powerful, humans can choose to act in good and evil ways; and

Belief in a last day of judgment.

While many Christians and Jews can identify these tenets in their own religions, these are in fact the Six Pillars of Faith in Islam (more on this later on).

Religion offers many opportunities for you to learn and get involved, such as:

Studying your own religion;

Assisting in services;

Assisting in religious training;

Assisting in fund raising;

Participating in charitable activities;

Writing newsletters;

Developing/maintaining web sites;

Participating in affiliated organizations;

Caring for church/synagogue/mosque/meeting house properties;

Working in youth programs.

It can also be helpful to study religions other than your own (assuming you have one, and even if you don't, it can still be helpful to understand why religion is so important to some people). Take Islam, for instance. Having an understanding of the history and drivers of the Islamic faith can be very helpful in understanding some of the dynamics of today's events and the pressures that will shape tomorrow's world.

## Resources for Getting Started

*World Religions: The Great Faiths Explored & Explained*
John Bowker
DK Adult, 2006

*The World's Religions: Our Great Wisdom Traditions*
Huston Smith
HarperOne, 1991

www.religionfacts.com
www.comparativereligion.com

# RENEW YOUR MARRIAGE VOWS

Opportunities: intellectual, social

Consider renewing your marriage vows. Given your years of experience your vow can express your love with a depth of understanding you didn't have at the first ceremony. This can be a very moving experience, not just for you and your spouse, but also for children, family and friends. It can be as formal/casual, religious/secular, simple/elaborate as you want to make it.

Consider revisiting your original honeymoon destination or perhaps the destination that you would have liked but couldn't afford.

## Resources for Getting Started

*Renew Your Marriage at Midlife*
Steve Brody
Perigee, 2008


www.idotaketwo.com/renewsing-wedding-vows.html

# RIVER TRACING (AND MORE) ────────

Opportunities: intellectual, physical

Live near a river or stream? Consider tracing its path from beginning to end. Where are its headwaters? What other rivers or streams contribute to it? Where does it terminate? How does it change with the seasons?

You might also investigate how the river or stream has been used over time, e.g. for drinking water, agriculture, industry, sewage disposal, transportation, power generation, fishing etc.

You might go further and investigate the quality of the river or stream. Has it been degraded by the uses to which it has been put? What can be done to reverse the degradation?

All of the above can make you an expert of sorts and perhaps become the basis of an article on the river for a local newspaper or journal, or perhaps even a book.

You might even decide to become a caretaker for the river and work for its well being.

## Resources for Getting Started

*Rivers of America*
Tim Palmer
Harry N. Abrams, Inc., 2006

*The Connecticut River*
Evan Hill
Wesleyan University Press, 1972

*The Chicago River: A Natural and Unnatural History*
Libby Hill
Lake Claremont Press, 2000

www.AmericanRivers.org

www.epa.gov/adopt/ (many good ideas)

http://water.usgs.gov (U.S. Dept. of the Interior/U.S. Geologic Survey site on water resources)

www.dnr.state.mn.us/adoptriver/index.html (example of what one state is doing)

Contact your local watershed or water district for additional information and opportunities.

## SENIOR ORGANIZATIONS

Opportunities: intellectual, social, physical

**AARP***:* If you are not already a member, you might consider joining AARP. AARP is a nonprofit membership organization focused on addressing the needs and interests of persons 50 and older. As a member you get access to:

Lots of good information and education about issues affecting folks over 50 with representation at the local, state and national levels on those issues;

Opportunities for community service;

Products and services designed for people over 50 plus;

A monthly magazine: *AARP: The Magazine*.

## Resources for Getting Started

AARP
601 E. Street, NW
Washington, DC 20049
Phone: (800) 424-3410 or (202) 434-2277
www.aarp.org

**Elderhostel**: An international nonprofit organization that sponsors "learning adventures" for people age 55 and older. Their programs include outdoor adventures to study culture, history and the natural environment, skill building programs, liberal arts and service learning (learning while helping others).

Elderhostel also sponsors the Elderhostel Institute Network that is a voluntary association of Lifelong Learning Institutes. The Institutes are community-based educational organizations, frequently associated with a college or university, that are focused on providing continuing educational opportunities for people of retirement age regardless of any previous levels of education.

## Resources for Getting Started

Elderhostel Phone: (877) 426-8056

www.elderhostel.org
www.elderhostel.org/ein/intro.asp

"Old people constitute America's biggest untapped and undervalued human energy source."

—Maggie Kuhn

**The Gray Panthers**:  The organization was founded 1971 by Maggie Kuhn and several other recently retired women who were facing problems associated with retirement: loss of the social status of being employed, loss of income and loss of opportunities for socialization. They evolved into a national advocacy group working on a wide variety of issues affecting older adults such as ageism and the need for nursing home reform as well as intergenerational issues. Their work continues today.

## Resources for Getting Started

Gray Panthers National Office
1612 K Street, NW
Suite 300
Washington, DC 20006
Phone: (800) 280-5362 or (202) 737-6637
www.graypanthers.org

**Senior Corps**:  An organization that connects folks age 55 and older with individuals and organizations that need their help. Examples of Senior Corps programs include:

*Foster Grandparents*, which connects volunteers age 60 and over with young folks who need their help and companionship;

*RSVP*, which matches volunteers 55 and older with a wide

range of service opportunities in their communities; and *Senior Companions*, which links volunteers age 60 and over with folks who are challenged with some of the basic tasks of daily living.

## Resources for Getting Started

Senior Corps
1201 New York Avenue, NW
Washington, DC 20525
Phone: (202) 606-5000
www.seniorcorps.org

**Seniornet**: A San Francisco-based nonprofit that provides educational technology support and discussion forums for folks age 50 and over, either online or at one of their over 240 Learning Centers across the U. S. and in other countries.

You will find discussion forums on over 500 topics, numerous book clubs and assistance with many computer-related topics ranging from how to change your wallpaper to how to fix software problems to how to build your own computer from scratch. You can peruse the site for free but you need to register (no cost) if you wish to participate in the discussion forums.

The *Wall Street Journal* in 2003 called Seniornet "the best online forum for retirees."

## Resources for Getting Started

www.seniornet.org

# SITTING

Opportunities: social

Yes, a retirement "activity" can be sitting on your haunches, but not in this book. Our area of interest in this section is sitting in the sense of minding, tending, taking care.

There are various types of sitting: baby, parent, home, pet, plants, mail and newspapers — almost any situation in which someone will be absent and someone or something needs tending to during that absence.

You can sit on a volunteer basis ("I'd love to watch over Benny the goldfish while you are in France."), for reciprocity ("You watch mine; I'll watch yours.") or for compensation.

The sitting depends on your time and temperament as well as your desire for income. Obviously more challenge is attached to tending children than to making sure the jade plant is watered and the cat's litter box is changed. The more responsibility you take on, the more likely the person for whom you are providing the sitting services will want to pay, if payment is appropriate.

If you desire to sit on a regular basis for income, it would be good to put together a resume with references that would demonstrate your experience and trustworthiness. As a pet sitter, you can even have your qualifications certified — see the petsitters.org Web site below.

Also, if you are caring for children or older adults, you may want to review the American Red Cross material referenced. While some of it is directed at teenagers who aspire to become babysitters, it is good advice for care providers of any age.

## Resources for Getting Started

*What to Expect Babysitters Handbook*
Heidi Murkoff
Workman Publishing, 2003

*Pet Sitting For Profit*
Patti Moran
Howell, 1997

www.redcross.org/services/hss/care

www.petsitters.org

# SNOWSHOEING ─────────────────────────

Opportunities: social, physical

For many of us, snow skiing – alpine and/or cross-country – has been and may still be, part of our lives. But as we age, icy slopes and the need to dodge snow boarders, tends to diminish some of the attraction of alpine skiing. Cross-country skiing remains great exercise and is easily accessible as long as one is reasonably fit. (See also Cross-country Skiing.)

But what if you don't have skiing skills (and don't wish to try to acquire them) and/or you still want to get out in the snow, have some fun, enjoy the outdoors and get some excellent exercise to boot? If you can walk, you can snowshoe.

Snowshoes enable you to walk on the snow by providing a large deck surface that helps you "float" on the snow. The modern snowshoe is quite light and yet its binding provides good support for your feet and ankles. The underside of the snowshoe usually has a serrated bar or crampons to provide extra grip going up or down hill or on icy sections (though in years of snowshoeing I have yet to experience any significant slippage; a larger challenge — for me at least — is not stepping on my own feet). If you are really ambitious, some manufacturers even make "running" snowshoes.

In many cases the snowshoes are all you need to get going. If you are going to be traveling on rugged terrain, you might want to consider using a pole or poles with baskets (the baskets — round appendages on the bottom of the poles — help keep the pole from sinking too deeply into the snow).

Many places in snow country will rent snowshoes and may provide access to snowshoe trails. But a real attraction to snowshoeing is that you can just go out your back door. Anywhere you can walk — parks, golf courses, woods, etc. — you can snowshoe.

## Resources for Getting Started

*The Snowshoe Experience*
Claire Walter
Storey Publishing, 2004

www.atlassnowshoe.com
www.tubbssnowshoes.com
www.carlheilman.com/snowshoe.html

# SOAP MAKING

Opportunities: intellectual, social

The origins of soap making are a bit murky. There is evidence the ancient Babylonians had a use for animal fats boiled with ashes, but it is unclear if it was for cleansing or hairdressing. The ancient Egyptians used fats with salts for medicinal purposes and perhaps for cleansing.

The Romans clearly used soap for cleaning clothes and personal hygiene. Legend has it that soap was discovered by women washing clothes in the Tiber River at the base of Mount Sapo. There was a temple on Sapo where animals were sacrificed. Rainwater would wash animal fat and ashes from sacrificial fires down the mountainside to the river where it created a foamy substance that facilitated the clothes washing process. From Mount Sapo comes our technical term for making soap: saponification.

Making soap can be interesting and rewarding whether you are making it for your own use, for gifts for family and friends or for profit. You can get the colors, scents and shapes you desire; you can even mix in your choice of herbs and other botanicals.

In fact, you may have already made soap. If you have ever had to use a drain cleaner to free a greasy drain, you have made soap in the process. The drain cleaner reacts chemically with the greasy plug to make a soapy substance that can then be flushed away.

While our ancestors used animal and vegetable fats from the kitchen and lye obtained by leaching water through an ash-filled barrel to make soap, it is a lot easier for us. Soap making basically entails:

1.  Mixing lye into water;

2.  Mixing the result of 1) with a fat or fats, e.g. lard, butter, coconut oil, corn oil;

3.  Adding essential oils, herbs etc. of your choosing;

4.  Pouring the result of 2) and 3) into a mold;

5.  Removing the soap from the mold after cooling; and

6.  Letting it age a few weeks.

Detailed recipes are available from the resources listed below. You can also just type "soap making" into your browser, and you will find many good resources. A word of caution: you need to be very careful working with lye. Lye is caustic and can be damaging to certain substances, including you. Be sure to read and abide by all instructions for handling it safely.

## Resources for Getting Started

*The Soapmaker's Companion*
Susan Miller Cavitch
Storey Publishing, 1997

*Smart Soapmaking*
Anne Watson
Shepard Publications, 2007

www.colebrothers.com/soap
www.millersoap.com

# STAINED GLASS

Opportunities: intellectual, physical

Aren't some plain glass windows boring? Would you rather look through your window at your neighbor's house or through something more colorful? You want natural light in your bathroom, but do you want to leave the shade up?

Consider making your own stained glass window. You can design the window using crayons. Once you have it the way you want it, you will need from your craft store: colored glass, solder, a glass cutter, thin copper foil, a soldering gun, liquid flux, a pair of pliers, protective gloves and goggles. While it would be best to take a beginner's class or review a basic book or web site, the high level view of the process is as follows: cut the glass, edge the pieces with the copper foil, clean the foil with the flux and then solder the pieces together on both sides, and you have your window. You can also use stained glass to make trays, chessboards, sculptures, vases, boxes, mirror frames and all sorts of decorative stuff.

## Resources for Getting Started

*Stained Glass: Step by Step*
Patricia Ann Daley
Hard Books Press, 2003

*Stained Glass Crafting*
Donatella Zaccaria
Sterling Publishing, 1998
www.aisg.on.ca
www.stainedglass.info

# STAMP COLLECTING ———————————

Opportunities: intellectual, social

Stamps were invented in England about 1840. Prior to then, people who received mail had to pay for the delivery. The new system of stamps worked so well that it began to be adopted in the United States in 1847. It was not long before folks began to collect stamps — some for historical interest, some because of a link to an area of personal interest, and some for decorative purposes.

Historical, thematic and topical stamp collections are all popular. While you can collect regular, everyday postage stamps, many collectors focus on "commemoratives" — stamps that honor a date, invention, event, person, place or other subject matter. Over 500,000 distinct stamps have been issued by countries around the world since 1840; there are plenty of specialization areas from which to choose.

## Resources for Getting Started

*The Stamp Collector's Bible*
Stephen R. Datz
House of Collectibles, 2002

www.stamps.org (American Philatelic Society)

www.stamplink.com

# SURFING

Opportunities: social, physical

When Old King Neptune's raising Hell
and the breakers roll sky high,
let's drink to those who can ride that stuff
and to the rest who are willing to try.

—John "Doc" Ball

John "Doc" Ball was a retired dentist and photographer who surfed into his 90s. I am not suggesting anyone follow his example, but there are lots of folks with gray hair who take up or continue to enjoy the sport.

British Captain James Cook reported on natives in the Sandwich Islands (aka Hawaii) riding the surf on canoes and boards or simply body surfing. The Hawaiians called it *he è nalu* or "wave sliding." The Brits called it "surf bathing."

George Freeth, a Hawaiian of royal Hawaiian and Irish ancestry, brought surfing to Redondo Beach, California in 1907. The first California surfing championship was held in 1928. People have been trying to catch a wave and an endless summer ever since.

If you don't feel up to surf boarding, and you don't mind getting some sand in your suit, body surfing can be a lot of fun also. And if you don't live near the ocean (or even if you do), you can try windsurfing or boardsailing.

## Resources for Getting Started

*Learn to Surf*
James McLaren
The Lyons Press, 1997

*Surfing — The Ultimate Pleasure*
Leonard Lueras
Workman Publishing, 1984

www.surfing-waves.com
www.legendarysurfers.com

# TAI CHI

Opportunities: physical

Tai Chi is a form of physical training in which you perform various movements in a slow, smooth, graceful fashion. The movements are designed to build flexibility, balance and strength, and to stimulate the flow of the vital life force — Chi — through our body. Taken together, the movements seem a bit like a slow motion "yoga dance" or perhaps a "moving meditation." It originated in China, but is now practiced around the world.

## Resources for Getting Started

*Step-By-Step Tai Chi*
Aster Lam Kam-Chuen
Fireside, 1994

*Beginning T'Ai Chi*
Tri Thong Dang
Tuttle, 1994

www.chebucto.ns.ca/Philosophy/Taichi

# TERRARIUMS

Opportunities: intellectual

Have you ever wanted to create your own little world? You can. A terrarium is a little world — a self-contained eco-system of plants and other creatures as you desire. In many ways it is the land-based equivalent of an aquarium.

The concept for a terrarium first came to Nathaniel Ward in 1827. Nathaniel lived in London, England that, at the time, had terrible air pollution issues. While trying to grow some moths under them he noticed a fern growing and thriving under one of the domes — something it could not do outside. He proceeded to construct the first terrarium, and thus glass cases used for this purpose, particularly those with a Victorian appearance, came to be called, "Wardian Cases," in honor of Nathaniel.

Terrariums can be diminutive worlds the size of a small vase, floor-to-ceiling glass cases, or anything in between. More frequently they will be enclosed systems. For a typical terrarium, you could start with a glass enclosure (at least the front should be glass – you want to be able to see inside), add soil (base, substrate and top soil materials) which you can landscape as you wish, and then add wood branches, plants, rocks, leaves, twigs, lichens and mosses, etc. as you deem appropriate for the world you are creating. Alternatively, you might create a desert terrarium and thus would focus more on sand, rocks, cacti and tumbleweed.

Terrarium life forms are not restricted to plants. You can add insects and it becomes an insectarium, reptiles result in a reptarium, a simulated rain forest is a paludarium and if you combine elements of both an aquarium and terrarium you get a riparium. So many choices! It is probably a good idea to start small, and perhaps think contrarian with respect to your local climate, e.g. if you live in a cold wet area, perhaps you'd like a desert; if you live in a desert (or Iowa), perhaps you'd like a rainforest.

## Resources for Getting Started

*Tabletop Gardens*
Rosemary McCreary
Storey Publishing, 2002

www.hort.purdue.edu/ext/HO-13.pdf

www.blackjungle.com

# THEATER

Opportunities: intellectual, social

The origins of theater date back at least to 534 B.C. and an individual called "Thespis" who won a play competition that year honoring the Greek God Dionysus. From Thespis we get our word "thespian" to describe the dramatic arts.

The ancient Greeks focused on *tragedies* (serious plays frequently dealing with conflict between a character and some higher power) and *comedies* (satires, characterizations and critiques that tended to make people laugh). The two masks (one smiling, the other in tears) associated with drama are the symbols of the Greek goddesses or Muses of comedy (Thalia) and tragedy (Melpomene).

Other genres of theatrical performance have been added over the years, e.g. musicals, melodramas, operas, mysteries, farce, giving us lots from which to choose. The Greeks and later the Romans built large stone outdoor theaters for their performances. While many performances today still take place outdoors, we also have the options of roofs, central heating/air conditioning and padded seats to enhance our enjoyment.

While Broadway rightly deserves its fame for its theatrical productions, there are opportunities all over the country to view Broadway shows on tour, shows that will eventually be on Broadway, shows that will never make it to Broadway but are excellent nonetheless. In addition, there are reprisals of Broadway shows, Shakespeare, Greek tragedies and comedies, Arthur Miller, Anton Chekhov, Henrik Ibsen, Neil Simon and offerings from thousands of other playwrights in thousands of settings, such as:

Your nearest big city's equivalent of Broadway;

Regional theaters;

Summer stock;

Town theaters;

Colleges;

High Schools.

This list generally reflects the descending level of cost associated with attending. Check your newspapers or web listing for information on performances, or you can go to the web site listed below for help in finding performance information at many venues other than at the high school level.

While you can certainly attend a performance on your own, why not make it a group event with dinner afterwards for discussion?

## Resources for Getting Started

*History of the Theatre*
Oscar Brockett, Franklin Hildy
Allyn & Bacon, 2007

*Our Musicals, Ourselves*
John Jones
Brandeis, 2004

www.theatermania.com (performance information)

(See also Acting.)

# THEME PARTIES ————————————

Opportunities: intellectual, social

Parties are almost always fun and most of us have hosted or attended our share of traditional holiday (New Year's, Labor Day, Halloween, Xmas, etc.) and event (retirement, Super Bowl, graduation, etc.) themed festivities. Since we have those "down pat," perhaps it is appropriate to try some new ones or revisit some very old ones. For excuses to party, consider, in calendar year order:

*Ides of March* (March 15) – This is the date of the assassination of Julius Caesar in 44 BC by a group of Roman senators who feared he was on his way to making himself King (or perhaps they were just jealous). Anyway, great excuse for an Italian dinner and to raise a toast to a great statesman, general and author: Hail Caesar! (NB: People still put flowers on his grave in Rome.)

*Spring* (or Vernal) *Equinox* (about March 21) – the day and night are of equal length. The days will be getting longer. We are passing from winter into spring. Celebrate the passing and/or the arrival. Plant some herb seeds and toast the fertility of the land!

*Arbor Day* (Last Friday in April at the Federal level, the various states have their own dates) – celebrate trees! Have a party around a tree planting. See Trees in this book for lots of reasons why trees are worth celebrating.

*Summer Solstice* (about June 22) – the sun is at its high point in the sky; it is the longest day of the year. We are warm and life is good. We take time off to relax from our labor. Toast the sun!

*Honey Moon* (midsummer – pick your date) – the mid-summer moon has been called the "Honey Moon" after the honey-based mead drunk at June weddings and betrothal ceremonies in medieval times. Toast the moon and love!

*Fall* (or Autumnal) *Equinox* (about September 22) – day and night are equal in length again. Nights will be getting longer and the days colder. The harvest is in. It is time to get together with friends and strengthen our spirits in anticipation of winter. To the harvest and friendship!

*Grape Harvest Festival* (early October – pick your date). The harvest is in and crushed. Fermentation is underway. Time to toast the grape and its wonderful liquid derivative!

*Winter Solstice* (about December 22) — the shortest day of the year. The days will be getting longer, the sun rising higher in the sky. Spring is promised to us. Celebrate the passing of the long, dark nights and the anticipation of the coming of warmth and new life from the earth!

Of course, if you live in the southern hemisphere much of the above must be reversed.

Anyway, you get the idea — there is always something to celebrate. If you need an excuse to party on a particular day the web site listed under Resources can provide you with one for every day of the year!

## Resources for Getting Started

www.earthcalendar.net/index.php

# TIN CRAFT

Opportunities: intellectual, physical

Do you recycle your tin and aluminum cans? Toss them out? How about reusing them to make decorations or useful objects such as lanterns, bird feeders, sconces, candlesticks, bookmarks, jewelry, match holders, etc.?

You can make many of these items with just a can opener, a set of snips, pliers, a small hammer and an awl. Add paint, chisels, cement, wire and solder and your creative boundaries become almost unlimited.

## Resources for Getting Started

*Tin Craft*
Fern-Rae Abraham
Sunstone Press, 1994

*The Fine Art of the Tin Can: Techniques and Inspiration*
Bobby Hanson
Sterling Publishing, 1999

www.specialtybottle.com
familycrafts.about.com/od/tincancrafts

---

# TOOL COLLECTING

Opportunities: intellectual, social

Just about every *thing* you own required one or more tools to make it. Tracing the history of tools helps trace the development of human industry. You may find it interesting to learn about this history and perhaps to own a bit of it. Rare tools may be interesting conversation pieces (try leaving a monkey wrench out on the coffee table) and perhaps the beginning of a valuable collection.

## Resources for Getting Started

*Tools*
Garrett Wade Company
Simon & Schuster, 2001
(not about collecting, but plenty of good information)

*Collecting Antique Tools*
Herbert Kean
Astragal, 1990

www.tooltimer.com
www.mwtca.org

## TRAINS ————————————————————————————

Opportunities: intellectual, social

Trains offer many areas with which to get involved.

Learn their history as they evolved from horsepower to steam, diesel, electric and maglev and had an increasing impact on the industrial economy until the advent of good roads and the trucking industry.

Hike old train tracks and learn why they were built — many were purpose-built for mining, quarrying, hauling guano, factory supplies, lumber and the like.

Build model train layouts either indoors or out in your garden (if space and climate permit) and run model trains. This can be a lot of fun to share with the grandkids.

Collect train memorabilia — lanterns, switches, posters, number plates, signage. This can be interesting, both historically and decoratively.

Take a trip on a famous train service, such as:

Broadway Express (New York to Chicago);

City of New Orleans (Chicago to New Orleans);

Flying Scotsman (London to Edinburgh);

Orient Express (Paris to Vienna);

Hogwart's Express (If you can find the platform);

The Canadian (Toronto to Vancouver).

Or visit a railroad museum and/or take a ride on a classic train service. A directory can be found on the first web site listed.

## Resources for Getting Started

*The Great Book of Trains*
Brian Hollingsworth, Arthur F. Cook
Motorbooks International, 2006

*The Encyclopedia of Trains and Locomotives*
David Ross, Ed.
Thunder Bay Press, 2007

www.rrmuseumpa.org
www.trains.com (information on indoor and outdoor model trains, classic and modern day "real" trains and railroading history)

# TRAP/SKEET/SPORTING CLAY SHOOTING

Opportunities: intellectual, physical

Think you have good reflexes? A steady hand? Good eye-hand coordination? Ever watch a bird fly by and raise your hand pistol, follow its path, and pretend (bang!) to shoot it out of the sky? Sure, you probably wouldn't *really* want to shoot the poor bird, but the target practice aspect of it might have felt like fun – sort of a much more realistic arcade game.

Folks used to use real pigeons for recreational target shooting, but 100 or so years ago the "clay pigeon" (a disk made of pitch and chalk) came into use as a more humane replacement for the winged version. Shooting of clay pigeons is a popular recreational activity and an Olympic sport. A device called a "trap" is used to hurl the clay pigeon into the air and a shotgun is used to shoot at the pigeon. For increased challenge, two pigeons can be hurled forth at the same time. Depending on the size of the pigeon (s), the speed, angle and variety of ascent, and the positioning of the shooter, the type of shooting may be deemed Trap, Skeet or Sporting Clay.

Of course, if you prefer live birds, there is always quail shooting in Texas, but be sure to exercise caution and stay behind the shooter.

## Resources for Getting Started

*The Gun Digest Book of Trap & Skeet Shooting*
Richard Sapp
KP Books, 2004

www.nssa-nsca.com (skeet and sporting clay)
www1.shootata.com (trap)

# TRAVEL AND LEARN ———————————————

Opportunities: intellectual, social, physical
(depending on how you travel)

While you almost always learn something new on any trip you take, there are a variety of organizations that offer trips that have a particular focus on learning.

Elderhostel, for instance, is a not-for-profit organization providing educational travel programs called, "Learning Adventures," for folks 55 and older (and for their spouses, significant others, children and grandchildren).

There are approximately 8,000 programs per year on a very wide variety of subjects. There is a strong educational focus to the programs but no particular educational background is needed (and there are no tests, grades or homework!).

**Elderhostel** programs include travel, accommodations, meals, lectures, field trips, cultural excursions, gratuities, and medical or insurance coverage.

Elderhostel groups their programs into these categories:

*Traditional* – These programs provide opportunities to study diverse cultures, delve into ancient histories, study literature and art, and learn about modern peoples and issues.

*Exploring North America* – These programs trace various themes such as American Heritage, American Landscapes, Cultural Arts, Food & Wine, Houses & Gardens, National Parks, and Signature Cities through designated areas of the United States and Canada.

*Active Outdoor* – Learn while you hike, bike, canoe, sail, etc. Elderhostel will give you guidance on how much physical activity is involved in each program.

*Service* – These programs involve both learning and the opportunity to give something back to society. You can get involved with wildlife or marine research, protecting endangered species, assisting at a zoo, improving recreational areas and a wide range of other endeavors.

*Adventures Afloat* – Study art, history, culture and the environment from a floating classroom.

*Intergenerational* – Explore space travel, dinosaurs, rainforests, Alaska or the world of Harry Potter (and lots of other worlds) with your grandchildren.

## Resources for Getting Started

Elderhostel
Phone: (877) 426-8056
www.elderhostel.org.

**Major museums** also offer travel programs that are connected to the museum's area of expertise. Frequently these trips are led by members of the museum's professional staff who may provide lectures and perspective throughout the trip. Because of their design features, these trips may be a bit more expensive on average than the Elderhostel programs mentioned previously. Some programs may require you to become a member of the museum to be able to take advantage of them.

**The American Museum of Natural History:**

Hidden India: A tented Safari through Central India

Mexico's Copper Canyon

The Ancient Silk Road (China)

Treasure Islands: Samoa, Tonga and Niue

Polar Bear Watch

Rainforest, Reefs and Ruins (Belize)

## Resources for Getting Started

American Museum of Natural History
Phone: (212) 769-5700
www.amnh.org

The **Metropolitan Museum of Art** offers these representative programs:

> Buddhism Triumphant: Burma and Vietnam
>
> Cuba (the Met has a license from the US Gov. to take tours to Cuba)
>
> Treasures of Britain and Ireland
>
> Princely Domains: Prague to Berlin
>
> Temples and Treasures of Japan
>
> Russian Winter Arts

## Resources for Getting Started

> Metropolitan Museum of Art
> Phone: (212) 650-2110
> www.metmuseum.org

Representative programs from the **Natural History Museum of Los Angeles County:**

> Inner Tibet
>
> Galapagos Islands
>
> Dinosaur Excavations in Kansas or China
>
> Brazil's gem-producing regions
>
> Viking Iceland
>
> Treasures of Florence

# Resources for Getting Started

Natural History Museum of Los Angeles County
Phone: (212) 763-3350
www.nhm.org

Representative programs from the **Smithsonian Institution**:

Mongolia: Land of the Nomad

Hidden Treasures of the Po River

Peru: Empires of Gold

Journey of Odysseus

Essence of Scotland

Mysteries of Morocco

# Resources for Getting Started

Smithsonian Institution
Phone: (877) 338-8687
www.smithonianjourneys.org

Representative programs from **National Geographic Society**:

In Search of Machu Picchu

A Taste of Umbria

Botswana Hemingway Safari

Alaska's Inside Passage

Ireland Biking

Mysteries of Egypt

## Resources for Getting Started

National Geographic Society
Phone: (888) 966-8687
www.nationalgeographic.com

Representative programs from the **American Heritage Institute:**

Over There: An Exploration of the American Expeditionary Forces During World War I in France

100 Years Of Flight: A Celebration of Aviation in Britain

Victory in Europe: World War II—from Bastogne to Berchtesgaden

St. Petersburg Tercentennial: 300 Years of Military History

The Industrial Revolution In England: The Places Where the Modern  World Was Born

## Resources for Getting Started

American Heritage Institute
Phone: (800) 556-7896
www.americanheritage.com

**Academic Travel Abroad** is a major organizer of educational travel. ATA partners with various institutions, as well as the alumni associations of a number of colleges and universities such as UCLA, Harvard, Yale and the University of Michigan to provide a wide variety of interesting programs.

You can visit their website, click on the part of the world in which you are interested, review a listing of available tours including day-by-day travel itineraries, and then obtain registration information.

## Resources for Getting Started

Academic Travel Abroad
www.academic-travel.com
Phone: (800) 556-7896

# TREES

Opportunities: intellectual, physical

"I think that I will never see/ A poem lovely as a tree" are the first two lines of the well-known poem "Trees" by Joyce Kilmer. Joyce (a man) was a WWI hero and has a park named after him in Brooklyn, New York. It is planted with oak trees.

Trees do much for us in addition to being lovely things on which to gaze, then wax poetic. They remove carbon dioxide (a "greenhouse" gas) and other gaseous pollutants from the air and return oxygen; they provide shade and cooling; reduce soil erosion and flooding; add to our property values; provide homes for squirrels, birds and insects; give us wood for construction, furniture, paper and heating; screen unsightly views and reduce noise; act as wind and snow breaks; feed us with fruit, nuts and maple syrup; are an important source of pharmaceutical products; give us opportunity for exercise as we rake leaves in the fall that is then used for mulch in our flower gardens.

Trees are also valuable as commemoratives of loved ones — the dogwood tree in front of our house was given to us by our neighbors in memory of our Golden Retriever, Simon, whose ashes help nourish the tree. It is known in the neighborhood as "Simon's Tree."

According to the USDA Forest Service, in 50 years, one tree generates over 30,000 dollars worth of oxygen, recycles over 35,000 dollars worth of water, and removes over 60,000 dollars worth of air pollution.

So consider planting trees as part of your legacy to the world.

You can also learn about trees. For instance, what trees grow in your area? How do they reproduce and distribute their seeds? (Hint: squirrels and birds help.) Can you find any baby trees to nurture? What value do they add — as a species or simply as being that particular tree in that particular location? How long do they live? How big do they get? Are they healthy, etc.? Your increased knowledge may be fertilizer for further plantings.

## Resources for Getting Started

*Trees of North America*
C. Frank Brockman, Rebecca Marrilees
Golden Guides for St. Martin's Press, 2001

*The Tree Doctor*
Daniel Prendergast, Erin Prendergast
Firefly Books Ltd., 2003

*Successful Tree Planting*
George Stroempl
Thomson Delmar Learning, 2006

www.arborday.org/learn
www.cnr.vt.edu/dendro/Forsite/Idtree.htm
www.treesaregood.com/treecare/tree_benefits.aspx
www.treelink.org
www.arborday.org (great info and a place to order tree seedlings)
www.plantit2020.org/about.html (non-profit tree-planting foundation w/excellent info)

# UMPIRE

Opportunities: intellectual, social, physical

Love sports? Love helping young people? Always wanted to be a judge? Be an ump!

Little leagues, town leagues, schools and other organizations need help with umpiring games — baseball, basketball, hockey, boxing, lacrosse, football, wrestling, water polo, you name it. But first, you need to:

Know the game and the rules;

Know how to position yourself in relation to the players;

Be able to make firm, accurate and decisive judgments;

Stand firm in controversial situations;

Acknowledge and correct your mistakes (not withstanding the above); and

Not permit the emotional comments or antics of players, coaches or parents to shake your poise.

## Resources for Getting Started

www.naso.org/BeOfficial (how to become an official)

www.abua.com (Amateur Baseball Umpires Association)

www.littleleague.org/umpires

www.lacrosse.org/official

# VETERANS' ORGANIZATIONS

Opportunities: social

A listing of veterans' organizations can be found in Appendix D. Many of these hold periodic conventions, produce publications with topics of interest for their memberships, lobby on behalf of members' well being and provide opportunities for social interaction.

## Resources for Getting Started

www1.va.gov/vso

# VOLUNTEERING

Opportunities: intellectual, social, physical

"The great use of life is to spend it
on something that will outlast us."

—William James

"It is one of the most beautiful compensations
of this life that no man can sincerely try
to help another without helping himself."

—Ralph Waldo Emerson

Volunteering is the chance to make a difference, to give back, to help others in need. It takes many forms, from fairly structured assignments to informal helping of neighbors. With older adults living longer and healthier, many are looking for volunteer opportunities in their post-work lives. There are many nonprofit organizations, churches, hospitals, schools looking for help. Fortunately there are also groups and web sites to help bring the volunteers and those who need them together.

Consider several factors when deciding what volunteer opportunities you might wish to take on.

First — is there a cause or mission you deeply care about? For example, if homelessness is of major concern to you, look into volunteering at homeless shelters or soup kitchens. If literacy and children strike a chord, think about tutoring or mentoring programs. And if, like the author's wife, you care about nursing home residents and like dogs, then pet therapy might be right for you. Whatever the cause, you'll find that volunteering for an agency or group that works in support of an issue or cause you care about will probably make that volunteer experience more meaningful and rewarding.

Second — how much time do you want to spend? This is one of the first questions volunteer groups will ask. Is it an hour a week or several days a month? Some volunteer jobs require more of a commitment. For example, Experience Corps, a nonprofit based in Washington, D.C. that pays 1800 older adults small stipends to tutor school children in 14 cities requires at least 15 hours per week. Their volunteers rave about the program.

Other factors to consider:

Do you want to work in a team or alone?

Do you want or need a stipend?

Do you prefer episodic or scheduled assignments?

Are challenging/meaningful assignments available?

Does the organization or agency provide training and support to its volunteers?

Nonprofits realize that the coming retirement of the baby boomer generation — the 76 million born between 1946 and 1964 — presents a wonderful opportunity to engage a large cohort in productive and meaningful service to help address community needs. However, some agencies are more ready and able than others to accommodate flexible volunteer schedules and other volunteer preferences. And in some cases, the staff of nonprofits may find your skill sets intimidating (particularly if you are volunteering to do what they get paid to do). So do your homework and proceed gently.

## Resources for Getting Started

*Prime time: How baby boomers will revolutionize retirement and transform America*
Marc Freedman
Public Affairs, 2002.

*Volunteer USA*
Andrew Carroll
Fawcett Columbine, 1991

*You Can Make A Difference!*
Marlene Wilson
Volunteer Management Associates, 1990

(See also Appendix E for additional volunteering considerations and opportunities.)

# WALKING

Opportunities: social

Walking is great for you! Among other things, it:

Expends calories and helps reduce/keep off excess weight (you burn about half a calorie per pound of body weight per minute just sitting and thinking deep thoughts – if you do your thinking while taking a brisk walk, you can more than triple your calorie expenditure);

Benefits your cardiovascular health and function;

Reduces your risk of diabetes;

Can help improve your mood and avoid depression;

Can help avoid the likelihood of falls by improving balance;

Gets you in contact with a more diverse environment;

Provides opportunities for social interaction;

Reduces the use of hydrocarbons (if you walk vs. driving); and

Is simply enjoyable in its own right.

## Resources for Getting Started

Good sneakers or walking shoes.
Sensible clothing.
Open the door and off you go!

# WEATHER

Opportunities: intellectual

Ever wonder what causes the wind or why it comes from a particular direction? Why there are so many different types of clouds? What makes air pressure higher or lower, and why does it matter? What is the significance of warm or cold fronts — other than perhaps things getting somewhat warmer or colder? What makes some weather — thunderstorms, tornadoes, hurricanes — so destructive? Ever wonder why your TV weather person gets it so wrong up from time to time? And, yes, just why is it the sky is blue?

Ever wish you could understand what causes your weather and learn to predict the near-term outlook on your own? You can!

We live in an ocean of air. Like the watery oceans, it is relatively warm in some places, cooler or cold elsewhere; it has currents, swirls and eddies; it is almost always in motion; it is denser in some places than in others; sometimes it is clear, other times murky; things float in it — clouds, birds, balloons.

The basic causes of our weather — heat from the sun, the different rates at which earth and water absorb and release heat, rotation of the earth, the round shape of the earth and its seasonal tilt toward the sun, humidity and topography — are relatively easy to get your mind around. How they work together or in opposition to each other is what makes weather prediction interesting and a challenge.

You can learn how weather works, learn how to "read" clouds and what they portend, learn to interpret weather maps and make your own forecasts. While this can be fun and educational in its own right, if you are involved in boating, flying or other activities, knowledge of the weather can add to your safety as well as your enjoyment.

## Resources for Getting Started

*Meteorology*
Joseph Moran, Michael Morgan
Prentice Hall, 1997

*Mariner's Weather*
William Crawford
W.W. Norton, 1992

www.weather.gov
www.noaa.gov (*National Oceanic and Atmospheric Administration*)
www.cirrus.sprl.umich.edu/wxnet (*Large collection of weather links from The University of Michigan)*

# WEIGHTLIFTING (STRENGTH TRAINING)

Opportunities: physical

Our muscles are important for our normal daily activities but they also play major roles in controlling weight and supporting stamina, balance, flexibility and good posture.

Left on its own, our muscle mass tops out at about age 30 and then begins a decline which accelerates as we get into our 50s. The key is not to leave it on its own. It is best to intervene on your own behalf, and build and maintain your muscles.

You don't need to join a gym to do this. You don't even need dumbbells. There are strength-building exercises you can do in your home with no equipment at all. As you make progress, you may want to add some free weights to help you make greater progress.

Working with weights does not turn fat into muscle. As you build muscles (a separate substance which burns more calories than fat), there is less room on your frame for fat. If you don't maintain your muscles, they will burn fewer calories which means the calories you do consume (assuming equal intake and cardiovascular exercise) are free to build fat.

As mentioned at the beginning of this book, you need to make your own decision as to whether strength training or any other activity mentioned here is appropriate for you. If you have any doubts about what is appropriate for you, you should check with your doctor.

## Resources for Getting Started

*Fitness Over Fifty*
National Institute on Aging
W.W. Norton and Company, 2003

*Strength Training Past Fifty*
Wayne Westcott, Thomas Baechle
Human Kenetics Publishers, 1997

*Strength Training for Seniors*
Michael Fekete
Hunter House, 2006

# WINE

Opportunities: intellectual, social, physical

"We hear of the conversion of water into wine at the marriage in Cana as of a miracle. But this conversion is, through the goodness of God, made every day before our eyes. Behold the rain which descends from heaven upon our vineyards, and which incorporates itself with the grapes, to be changed into wine; a constant proof that God loves us, and loves to see us happy."

—Benjamin Franklin

As with so many things agricultural, winemaking probably originated in Mesopotamia (between the Tigris and Euphrates Rivers in what is now Iraq). Clay jars dating to about 5,000 BC and containing wine residue have been found in the Zagros Mountains, just to the east of the Mesopotamian plain. Winemaking spread with human migration from the region and along the trade routes.

Early wines were quite crude compared to what we know today. Wines were fermented in open vats and stored in animal skins or poorly sealed amphorae. Because spoilage was an issue, most wines were drunk without much in the way of aging. In those days, wine was flavored with honey or herbs and usually cut with water since the basic wine was thick and syrup-like.

Grape cultivation prospered under the ancient Romans as more was learned about controlled fermentation, filtering and effective storage techniques. While winemaking declined with the decay of the Roman Empire, church monasteries kept the art alive due to their need for sacramental wine. As the Western World emerged from the "Dark Ages" wine emerged as well, evolving into the wide variety of offerings so many of us so enjoy today.

Other than simply enjoying the fruits of the winemaker's efforts, what else can we "do" with wine in retirement? Many things.

**Learning about wine** is one of the things that makes wine fun — it comes in endless varieties. Even the same wine from the same producer can vary significantly from year to year. What causes this great variety?

The type or types of grapes used to make the wine, e.g. catawba, cabernet sauvignon, chardonnay, sauvignon blanc, riesling, provide the foundation for the wine.

The soil in the vineyard adds character — grapes need water, sunlight and warmth to mature; rocky soils and sloping fields will let water drain more easily than dense soils and flat fields, so rocky and dark colored soils will hold heat better.

The climate, e.g. temperature ranges, rainfall, hours of sunlight, etc., contribute to the maturation process.

Crushing and fermentation techniques are part of the equation as well. And let's not forget the length of fermentation, filtration techniques, storage (stainless steel and/or various types of wood barrels), length of storage (months to years), blending and bottling.

Increased knowledge can add to your enjoyment of the final product and help you to assess its characteristics once you have popped the cork.

## Resources for Getting Started

*Windows on the World Complete Wine Course*
Kevin Zarly
Sterling, 2005

*Wine for Dummies*
Ed McCarthy, Mary Ewing-Mulligan
For Dummies, 2003

**Visiting wine country/wineries** to learn first hand how wine is made can be fun. This can be particularly interesting during the crushing season when there is a lot of activity and the smell of must (freshly pressed grapes) is in the air. Most larger wineries offer tours, tasting rooms and the opportunity to purchase at a reasonable price.

If you have a favorite wine — say, the pinot noirs of Oregon's Willamette valley — perhaps you might plan a trip to get to know the region and some of the wineries. It can be nice when opening a bottle to reflect back to when you walked in the winery's vineyard, toured the production facilities and saw all the barrels of wine resting in the storage facilities. If Oregon is a bit far for your travel budget, there are wineries in all 50 states.

If you are fortunate enough to be able to travel to other countries, a bit of research could lead you to wineries during your trip. Most non-tropical countries have wineries. Even if you don't visit the wineries be sure to try some of the local wines to learn about them and see if any might be added to your favorites list.

**Make wine**? Yes, you can do it!! (This is based on the writer's personal experience.)

You don't need a vineyard or even a wine barrel. If our forebears could make wine in open vats with yeast blown in by nature and store it in animal skins, you can make in plastic jugs and store it in bottles. There are books and kits that can help you do it. (See also below.) The (oversimplified) process involves mixing fruit that you crush (or grape juice that you order from a supplier) with boiling water and sugar, adding a few other ingredients including wine yeast, allowing the mixture to ferment (turning the sugar into alcohol), bottling and then aging. It is a bit more involved than that but less involved than some dinners I've made.

In most states you can make up to 100 gallons per year, if you are making wine for home consumption and are over 21.

## Resources for Getting Started

*Home Winemaking Step-By-Step*
Jon Iverson
Stonemark, 2000

*Joy of Home Winemaking*
Terry Garvey
Collins, 1996

www.allamericanwineries.com/AAWMain/locate.htm (info on wineries in all 50 states)

www.pressedforwine.com

www.winemaking.jackkeller.net (much guidance)

www.eckraus.com/index.htm (wine making kits and guidance)

Whether you buy or make your wine, you may find a **wine cellar** to be useful (fewer trips to the store, good selections for meal time, hostess gift in easy reach, place to store nice wines you wish to age). A wine cellar can be as simple as a corner in one of your basement closets or as elaborate as your imagination can make it.

What you are trying to accomplish with a wine cellar (in addition to simple storage) is a dark (no direct sunlight), cool (under 65 degrees F), humid (humidity greater than 50 percent) and stable (no big temperature variations) environment to protect the wine from premature aging. Depending on where you live your cellar may need cooling or humidification (The author's southern New England basement works fairly well all on its own.)

## Resources for Getting Started

*All About Wine Cellars*
Howard Goldberg
Running Press, 2004

www.cellarnotes.net/storing_wine.html

Organize a **wine tasting** with your friends! You can ask folks to bring a white or a red, or one of each. You might assign each person to bring one varietal from different geographical areas, say a pinot grigio from California, Italy, Chile and Australia or perhaps pinot noirs from California, Washington, Oregon and New Zealand.

Provide glasses, some crackers, mild cheese and a sheet for judging each wine and take into account:

*Appearance* – color, hue, clarity

*Bouquet or "nose"* – floral, fruity, spicy, chocolate and the like

*Taste* – sweet/dry, full/medium/light-bodied, soft/crisp

*Finish* – short/long and complex

Put each bottle in a numbered bag, start with the white (if you are having both white and red) and enjoy! For an interesting "Bluffer's Guide" for use at a tasting look here: www.wineoftheweek.com/murray/blind1.html

If you prefer to purchase a wine tasting party instruction book and kit (bags, scoring sheets, blind labels etc.), they are also available.

## Resources for Getting Started

*The Wine Tasting Party Kit*
Eliza Bullock
Chronicle Books, 2005

*Wine Spectator's Ultimate Wine Tasting Kit*
Harvey Steiman
Running Press Publishers, 2004

www.winecountrygetaways.com/host.html (scoring sheets)
www.atime4wine.com/ratingsheet.htm (scoring sheets)

# WIRE CRAFT

Opportunities: intellectual, physical

Get wired!

Wire crafting can be both fun and functional. It is also easy to learn and inexpensive (as long as you avoid working with precious metals). It also requires few tools: a couple of pairs of needle-nosed pliers and a set of shears and off you go.

Projects could include baskets, jewelry, wall or window hangings, sculptures, tools, mobiles, vases or whatever your imagination can dream up. Check out the creativity in the gallery section of wire-magic below.

## Resources for Getting Started

*WIRE (Craft Workshop)*
Mary McGuire, Peter Williams
Southwater Publishing, 2002

*Decorative Wirework*
Jane Davis
Krause Publications, 2002

*Wire (Everyday Things)*
Susanne Slesin, et al
Abbeville Press, 1994

www.wire-magic.co.uk

# WOMEN'S ISSUES

Opportunities: intellectual, social

Female readers, perhaps you'd like to involve yourselves in issues affecting women (and others):

The Right to Choose

Body image

Breast cancer

Domestic abuse

Girls without mothers

Work and family

Superwoman syndrome (do it all perfectly with time to spare)

## Resources for Getting Started

www.research.umbc.edu/~korenman/wmst/links.html

www.state.gov/g/wi/

# WOOD BURNING

Opportunities: intellectual, physical

Remember going to camp as a child and being given a square piece of wood with a design on it and a wood-burning pen?

Well, maybe you don't remember. Okay, maybe you didn't go to camp. Whatever . . . Wood burning (pyrography) can be a lot of fun and provide an interesting outlet for your creative aspirations. You can decorate tables, boxes, lamps, bookends, planters, bracelets — literally anything made out of wood for use in your abode or for gifts for friends and family.

How many other wood burners do you know? Be unique!

## Resources for Getting Started

*Learning the Art of Pyrography*
Al Chapman
Schiffer Publishing, 1999

*Introduction to Pyrography: The Art of Woodburning*
Daniel Wright
Search Press, 2004

*Basic Woodburning*
Sue Waters, Joanne Tobey
Schiffer Publishing, 1994

www.carvingpatterns.com/projects/burn.htm

# WOODWORKING

Opportunities: intellectual, physical

You don't need to be an experienced carpenter with lots of tools to enjoy working with wood. Antique furniture, now selling for hundreds of thousands of dollars, was constructed with simple hand tools. In addition, many items can be constructed from kits in which much of the preliminary or difficult cutting has been done for you. Your author constructed a grandfather clock from a kit thirty years ago; it still runs and looks great.

You can start simple – boxes, bird houses or bookcases – and move on to other items if your interest grows. Suggestions include:

*Boxes*: Simple or more elaborate for jewelry, tea, pencils, bread, toothpicks, spare change, plants, or maybe even a Zen sandbox for contemplation (you can get a couple of stones, make a little rake, draw various patterns and reflect on the meaning of everything and nothing).

*Clocks*: Grandfather, shelf or wall. The focus here is on making the case. You can purchase the clock movement for installation into the case. If you might be interested in making the movement, see the section on "Clock Making."

*Bedroom furniture*: Beds are easier to construct than you might think; cabinets and chests are a bit more challenging.

*Benches*: How about something for your entryway to assist with changing your boots/shoes?

*Bookcases*: A not too difficult and useful project.

*Cabinets*: A bit more challenging but certainly doable.

*Cedar chest*: Bug-free clothes protection.

*Chairs and tables*: Can you get all the legs the same length?

*Children's furniture*: If you want to start with something "small."

*Cradles/cribs*: You might want to consider a kit.

*Desks*: Another good candidate for a kit if you are a beginner.

*Shelving*: Another good beginner project.

*Trunks*: Something in which to store the quilts, comforters and duvets.

*Wine storage*: Racks, bins, cellars are not difficult.

*Workbench*: On which to do your woodworking projects and whatever else you might think of.

Outdoor Items

*Bat house*: They eat mosquitoes

*Birdhouse*

*Bird feeder*

*Christmas*: Santa? Frosty? Sleigh and all the reindeer?

*Halloween*: Something to put the "trick or treaters" in the right frame of mind?

*Gazebo*
*Lawn/garden furniture*

*Picnic table*

*Planter*

*Storage shed*

Toys

*Dollhouse*

*Fort for the grandkids*

*Puppet theater*

*Rocking horse*

It has been noted that many great pieces of furniture (and all sorts of other items) have been constructed with only hand tools. While this is correct, you may well find that some equipment – probably beginning with a table saw and a sander – can greatly add to your enjoyment.

It is also very helpful to begin by reading about woodworking to help you sort out which projects are within your skill set and areas of interest. It is also important to learn about safety – obviously, things that can cut wood can cut you too.

## Resources for Getting Started

*The Complete Manual of Woodworking*
Albert Jackson, David Day
Knopf, 1996

*Building Small Projects*
Editors of Fine Woodworking
The Taunton Press, 2004

*Woodworking Basics*
Peter Korn
The Taunton Press, 2003

www.murrayclock.com
www.klockit.com (ideas on clock case projects)
www.pionet.net/~tomcox
www.woodworking.com/ww101start.cfm
www.woodmagazine.com (click on woodworking basics)
www.woodworking.org (lots of good info and links)

# WORLD AFFAIRS

Opportunities: intellectual, social

Are you interested in world affairs, politics, history, culture and geography? Would you like to hear from experts in these fields and have the opportunity to talk with them about major issues of the day? Consider joining one of the World Affairs Councils. These Councils are non-profit and non-partisan. Eighty-six Councils operate under the umbrella of the World Affairs Councils of America located in Washington, D.C. They sponsor a variety of programs and speakers each year across the country. Membership fees are modest, between twenty-five and seventy-five dollars.

## Resource for Getting Started

www.worldaffairscouncils.org (info for individual councils)

# WRITING

Opportunities: intellectual

This is a huge field with many subsets. I will not attempt to review all of them here. The point is this: There are ample opportunities and forums for all who have something to say and a willingness to say it. In addition to the traditional outlets like newspapers, magazines, book publishers and journals, the Internet and Print-On-Demand (POD), technology offers the opportunity to get your writing into the public domain quickly and easily.

POD enables you to publish books that may be intended for only a small circulation (say, your family, religious group or club) or books for which you are not able to rouse the interest of a traditional publisher. You might also try:

*Blogging* – an Internet web log of your views and perspectives. (See also Blogging.)

*Book reviews* – your views on books that you have read or perhaps a comparison of books on similar subjects.

*Fiction* – maybe the next James Patterson or J. K. Rowling lies buried deep inside you. Also, a POD possibility.

*Newsletters* – for your religious or interest group.

*Newspaper column* – your comments on favorite pastimes, politics, field of expertise, advice to the lovelorn, whatever.

*Non-fiction* – something in your area of expertise or an area you researched and want others to know about.

*Poetry* – short pieces for magazines or journals, or if you are more prolific, perhaps your own book. Another POD possibility.

*Restaurant reviews* – you could be "the clandestine diner."

*Concert, Movie or Theater reviews.*

## Resources for Getting Started

*Becoming a Writer*
Dorothea Brande
Jeremy Tarcher, 1981
(a good book to get you "going")

*100 Things Every Writer Needs to Know*
Scott Edelstein
Perigee Trade, 1999
(experienced insight)

*Writing Down the Bones*
Natalie Goldberg
Shambhala, 1986

www.fictionfactor.com (on-line magazine for fiction writers)
www.childrenswriter.com
www.thewriter.com
www.writersdigest.com

# YODELING

Opportunities: intellectual, physical

Why? Because you can. (John Denver learned how to yodel, why not you?)

It has been used not just by the Swiss and The Von Trapp Family Singers but also African Pygmies, cowboys around the world, various singers in Australia, Europe, the South Pacific and Latin America.

## Resources for Getting Started

Yodel-Ay-Ee-Oooo
Bart Plantenga
Routledge, 2003

www.yodelcourse.com

# YOGA

Opportunities: intellectual, social, physical

"Yoga is for everyone."
— Yogacharya B. K. S. Iyengar

I concur. (Full disclosure: the author of the material you hold in your hands took up yoga at age 55, somewhat overweight, somewhat stiff, somewhat out of alignment and subsequent to two lower-back surgeries and thirty-some-odd years of corporate existence. It's been great for me; I've seen it help many others.)

My definition of yoga would be "a practice directed at bringing mind and body into alignment and state of well-being." Other definitions might focus more on physical exercises, mental and spiritual peace or something more philosophical. If you would like to develop yourself in any of these areas, yoga can add real value.

Yoga exercises (*asanas*) will help you build flexibility, strength, balance. They can also help reduce stress and improve your breathing. If you want to also take it to a place more spiritual, that path is available.

While there are books, videos and web sites with yoga guidance, I suggest the best way to begin is with a class. Even if you have a room full of mirrors, you can't really see everything your body is doing as you practice *asanas*. An instructor can help guide you to a faster, more effective start and help you get the most out of your practice. Once you get the lay of the land you can replace or supplement the classes with videos or books, as you deem appropriate. My own view is that the classes are fun and help challenge you to try new things and take your practice to higher levels.

Check with your town, YM/YWCA, school system, senior center, hospitals, etc. for the availability of classes.

## Resources for Getting Started

*YOGA The Path to Holistic Health*
Yogacharya B. K. S. Iyengar
Dorling Kindersley, 2001

*The Everything Yoga Book*
Cynthia Worbey
Adams Media Corp, 2002

*Light on Yoga*
B. K. S. Iyengar, Yehudi Menuhin
Schocken, 1995

www.yogajournal.com/index.cfm
www.yoga.com

# YO-YO

Opportunities: intellectual, physical

Can you walk the dog? Hop the fence (a low one)? Rock the baby? Loop the loop? Reach for the moon? These and lots of other moves are all yo-yo tricks.

The yo-yo has been with us for at least 2,500 years and it is probably the second oldest toy in the world after the doll. The oldest yo-yos are from Greece and you can see examples of them at the Metropolitan Museum of Art in New York. The yo-yo was also the first toy in space but it presented some challenges because yo-yos function much differently in zero gravity.

Yo-yos can be fun gifts for the young people in your life, and since you'll want to show them how to use them and do some tricks, you will need one for yourself. If there are no young people in your life then you can impress your contemporaries (albeit at some risk of "reverting to childhood" jokes).

There are also yo-yo contests (they are part of some senior Olympic competitions), regional and national championships and even a yo-yo museum in Chico, California.

## Resources for Getting Started

*Yo-yo Tricks and Tips*
Consumer Guide editors
Consumer Guide, 1999

www.worldyoyocontest.com (check out the videos!)
www.spintastics.com/HistoryOfYoYo.asp
www.ayya.net

# ZEN

Opportunities: intellectual

Great doubt: great awakening.
Little doubt: little awakening.
No doubt: no awakening.

—Zen koan

Gives you something to think about, doesn't it?

Brief background: Zen is an evolved form of Buddhism. Buddhism is a religion based on the teachings of Buddha, aka Siddhartha Gautama, who lived in India about 500 BC. While there are various forms of Buddhism, in general Buddhists attempt to come to an understanding of true reality and achieve a state of liberation and enlightenment. They do this by trying to live in a moral fashion, generally based on the Golden Rule of "Do unto others as you would have them do unto you," meditating and seeking wisdom. It is possible for Buddhists to also be Christians, Jews or Muslims.

Zen evolved from India through China, Japan, Korea and Viet

Nam. Zen seeks to achieve enlightenment about the nature of reality by meditating on koans like the one at the beginning of this section. Koans are questions or statements made by Zen masters to help students of Zen step away from normal every-day life and come to an understanding of the reality that transcends that life. Here is another koan:

> One day as Manjusri stood outside the gate, the Buddha called to him, "Manjusri, Manjusri, why do you not enter?"
>
> Manjusri replied, "I do not see myself as outside. Why enter?"

And another . . .

> Nan-in, a Japanese master during the Meiji era (1868-1912), received a university professor who came to inquire about Zen.
>
> Nan-in served tea. He poured his visitor's cup full, and then kept on pouring.
>
> The professor watched the overflow until he no longer could restrain himself. "It is overfull. No more will go in!"
>
> "Like this cup," Nan-in said, "you are full of your own opinions and speculations. How can I show you Zen unless you first empty your cup?"

Zen posits that we can't understand true reality because we are too wrapped up in living our subjective reality. By meditating on the koans we try to break away from our subjective reality by freeing ourselves from rational thinking and thus find the transcendent true reality.

So, if you are focused on the question "What's it all about when you sort it out, Alfie?" Zen is probably not you. But if you aspire to enlightenment without any sorting, Zen may add value.

## Resources for Getting Started

*An Introduction to Zen Buddhism*
Daisetz Teitaro Suzuki
Grove/Atlantic, 1991

*Zen Mind, Beginner's Mind*
Shunryu Suzuki
Weatherhill, 1973

www.ordinarymind.com/koans_frameset.html (koans with commentary)

www.terebess.hu/english/zen.html (general information and koans for reflection)

(See also Philosophy.)

# IF YOU DO NOTHING ELSE ────────────

If you decide not to do any of the fun, interesting, educational, engaging activities reviewed in this book, please do consider addressing at least the following:

Brain Exercise and Training
Estate Planning
Exercise
Family Relationships
Goal Setting
Living Will
Memory Strengthening
Physical Exam

# Appendix A

## LIFE EXPECTANCY CALCULATORS

Here are some life expectancy calculators. They will probably produce differing results because they emphasize different factors such as family medical history or driving habits. Try several — you'll come away with a pretty good understanding of the factors that make for a longer or shorter lifespan.

www.moneycentral.msn.com/investor/calcs/n_expect/main.asp
(MSN Money Central)

www.nmfn.com/tn/learnctr--life events--longevity_game (Northwestern Mutual Financial Network)

www.gosset.wharton.upenn.edu/mortality/perl/CalcForm.html
(University of Pennsylvania Professors)

www.msrs.state.mn.us/info/age_cal.htmls

www.calculator.eons.com/calculator
(EONS website)

# Appendix B

## SENIOR OLYMPICS

*\*Open to Out-of-State Residents*
*\*\*Open to Out-of-State Residents, except Team Sports*

**Alabama Senior**
**Olympic Games\***
Gov. Comm. on
Phys Fitness & Sports
560 S. McDonough
Montgomery, AL 36130

**Alaska Senior Games\***
P.O. Box 57033
Fairbanks, AK 99705

**Arizona Senior Olympics\***
P.O. Box 33278
Phoenix, AZ 85067-3278

**Arkansas Senior Olympics\***
P.O. Box 1577
Hot Springs, AR 7102

**California Senior Games**
**Association\***
85 E. Holly St.
Pasadena, CA 91103

**Colorado Rocky Mountain**
**Senior Games\***
Greeley Senior Activity Center
1010 Sixth St.
Greeley, CO 80631

**Connecticut Senior Games\***
Connecticut Sports Management Group
290 Roberts St. Suite 301
E. Hartford, CT 06108

**Delaware Senior Olympics**
1121 Forrest Ave.
Dover, DE 19904

**Florida Senior Games
State Championships\*\***
 Florida Sports Foundation
2930 Kerry Forest Pkwy.
Tallahassee, FL 32309

**Georgia Golden Olympics\***
P.O. Box 958
Winder, GA 30680

**Hawaii Senior Olympics\***
1493 Halekoa Dr.
Honolulu, HI 96821

**Idaho Senior Games\***
1050 West State St.
Boise, ID 83702

**Illinois Senior Olympics\***
1601 North 5th St.
Springfield, IL 62702

**Indiana Senior Games\***
37 E. Main St.
Carmel, IN 46032

**Iowa Senior Games\***
3550 George M. Mills
Civic Pkwy.
West Des Moines, IA 50265

**Kansas Senior Olympics\***
Parks & Recreation of Topeka
1534 S.W. Clay
Topeka, KS 66604

**Kentucky Senior Games\***
Ashland Visitors Bureau
1509 Winchester Ave.
Ashland, KY 41101

**Louisiana Senior
Olympic Games\***
P.O. Box 14748
Baton Rouge, LA 70898

**Maine Senior Games\***
136 US Rt. 1
Scarborough, ME 04074

**Maryland Senior Olympics**
12900 Middlerook Rd.
GermanTown, MD 20879

**Massachusetts Senior Games\***
 Springfield College
263 Alden St.
Springfield, MA 01109-3797

**Michigan Senior Olympics\***
650 Letica Dr.
Rochester, MI 48307

**Minnesota Northland
Senior Games***
Lakes Area Recreation
720 Fillmore St.
Alexandria, MN 56308

**Mississippi Senior Olympics***
 Baptist Healthplex
102 Clinton Pkwy.
Clinton, MS 39056

**Missouri State Senior Games***
University of Missouri
1105 Carrie Francke Dr.,
Room 01
Columbia, MO 65211

**Montana Senior Olympics***
2200 Bridger Dr.
Bozeman, MT 59715

**Nebraska Senior Games***
18 E. 22nd St.
Kearney, NE 68847

**Nevada Senior Games***
3925 S. Jones Blvd.
#1123
Las Vegas, NV 89103

**New Hampshire Granite State
Senior Games***
11 Stagecoach Way
Manchester, NH 03104-5759

**New Jersey Senior Olympics***
New Jersey Senior Olympics
P.O. Box 271
Caldwell, NJ 07006

**New Mexico Senior Olympics**
P.O. Box 2690
Roswell, NM 88202-2690

**New York Empire State
Senior Games**
State Office Building
163 W. 125th St., 17th Floor
New York, NY 10027

**North Carolina Senior Games**
P.O. Box 33590
Raleigh, NC 27636

**North Dakota Senior Games**
No state games. Contact South
Dakota.

**Ohio Senior Olympics***
Dist. XI AAA
25 E. Boardman St.
Youngstown, OH 44503

**Oklahoma Senior Olympics***
1829 West Honolulu
Broken Arrow, OK 74012

**Oregon Senior Games**
No state games. Contact Washington.

**Pennsylvania Senior Games**
c/o Keystone State Games, Inc.
P.O. Box 1161
Wilkes-Barre, PA 18773-3131

**Rhode Island Ocean State
Senior Olympics***
200 Allens Ave
Providence, RI 02903

**South Carolina Senior
Sports Classic**
326 Townes Rd.
Columbia, SC 29210

**South Dakota Senior Games***
317 N Union
Madison, SD 57042

**Tennessee Senior Games**
512 Schooner Cove
Hermitage, TN 37076

**Texas Senior Games***
PMB 325
3501 Sycamore School Rd.
Fort Worth, TX 76133

**Utah Huntsman World
Senior Games***
1070 West 1600 South,
Ste. 103A
St. George, UT 84770

**Vermont Green Mountain
Senior Games***
131 Holden Hill Rd.
Weston, VT 05161

**Virginia Senior Games***
6372 Mechanicsville
Mechanicsville, VA 23111

**Washington DC
Golden Olympics**
1480 Girard St., NW
Suite 420
Washington, D.C. 20010

**Washington State
Senior Games***
2218 Vista Ave., SE
Olympia, WA 98501

**West Virginia Senior
Sports Classic***
602 Tennessee Ave.
Charleston, WV 25304

**Wisconsin Senior Olympics***
 SE Wisconsin Agency on Aging
125 N. Executive Dr., Ste. 102
Brookfield, WI 53005

**Wyoming Senior Olympics***
Campbell County Parks & Rec.
PO Box 937
Sheridan, WY 82801

# Appendix C

## COLLECTIBLES
### A List To Start You Thinking

**Autographs:** historical figures, entertainers, sports figures, politicians, musicians. www.autographcollector.com

**Barbed Wire:** there are many types. www.barbwiremuseum.com

**Baskets:** straw, wicker, bar, wooden. www.basketmakers.com/topics/collect/collectmenu.htm

**Bells:** metal, glass ceramic, school, house, religious, musical, dinner, et al. Pick them all or a subset. www.americanbell.org

**Books:** rare, first editions, signed, books about particular persons, places or subjects. www.tappinbookmine.com

**Bottles:** antique, colored glass, medicine, whiskey, wine, miniatures, etc. www.fohbc.com

**Buttons:** uniform, antique, painted, wooden, stone, glass, pearl, animals, sports. www.iwantbuttons.com/NBS

**Calculators:** purely mechanical, electro-mechanical, handhelds. www.vintagecalculators.com

**Cameras:** antique, still, movie, spy, instant, large format, wooden. www.antiquewoodcameras.com/links.htm

**Clocks:** wind up, weight-driven, wood, brass. www.nawcc.org

**Clothing:** (Certainly less expensive than collecting sports cars or fine art.)

**Coffee Grinders:** glass, wood, steel, wall-hung

**Coins** (See also coin collection)

**Coin-operated Machines:** penny arcade machines, old slots

**Comic Art Forms:** artwork, comic books. www.comicbooks.about.com

**Computers** (My TI still works and must be worth something!)

**Cuff Links:** historical, patriotic, gambling, financial, animals, enamel, cast. www.enamelcufflinks.com

**Decoys** www.oldwoodenduckdecoys.com

**Dolls** (inanimate variety)

**Doll Houses**

**Fish Lures and Flies**

**Fishing Poles and Reels**

**Firearms:** antique, by manufacturer or type

**Firefighting Memorabilia**

**Furniture:** antique or by function.

**Glass:** bottles, depression glass, art work, by color, by country.

**Greeting Cards:** vintage, by holiday.

**Hardware:** antique versions of anything you might find in a hardware store.

**Holiday Items:** pick your holiday.

**Jewelry**

**Key Chains**: rabbit foot, automotive.

**Kitchen Equipment:** antique or by function.

**Ladies' Hand Fans** (functional art work). www.handfanpro.com

**Lamps:** oil, kerosene, electric.

**Leather Goods**

**License Plates:** by state, historical in your state or others, vanity plates. www.alpca.org

**Knives:** kitchen, throwing, hunting, utility, combat, knives with special handles, etc. www.nationalknife.org

**Magazines:** vintage, of historical interest, themes.

**Maps and Charts**: antique or by subject matter.

**Marbles:** think of the "lost my marbles" jokes you can come up with! www.landofmarbles.com

**Match Books:** An English Chemist, John Walker, invented the friction match in 1826. Since then, match books and match boxes have depicted a huge array of subjects. Pick yours. www.hobbymaster.com

**Medical Tools**

**Military Insignia and Medals**

**Miniatures**: **of anything,** e.g. books, toys, bottles, furniture, tools.

**Movie Memorabilia:** costumes, pieces of sets, posters, opening night tickets or programs, cartoon stills, props.

**Music Boxes:** miniature, carousels, animated, antique. www.mbsi.org

**Musical Instruments:** probably not grand pianos (unless you have the space and budget), but perhaps another instrument you play or admire. Or if space is limited, you might consider harmonicas, kazoos, bells or whistles. www.oriscus.com/mi/collecting.asp

**Paintings**

**Paperweights:** Combine paper and breeze and guess what you need. The first paperweight was probably a rock, but things progressed from the functional to the decorative. www.paperweight.org

**Pens:** quill (made using a "pen knife"), fountain, space, ballpoint, dip pens.

**Pencils:** "lead" pencils actually use graphite for writing. Lead hasn't been used for over 400 years – funny how some names just hang on. Why are pencils yellow? Because in the 1800's the best pencil lead came from China, the color yellow was associated with royalty in China and the pencil manufacturers wanted to show their pencils were really intended for the most royal users. www.pencilpages.com

**Phonographs:** crank-up and early electrics.

**Photographs:** antique; of a particular place, person or event.

**Picture Frames:** leather, wood, mother or pearl, plaster.

**Playing Cards:** these probably originated in China; Muslims developed the four-deck suit; the French gave us hearts, diamonds, clubs and spades and Americans invented the Joker. www.cpccinc.org

**Political Memorabilia**

**Postcards:** places you've been or would like to go; your state or city; places your friends have gone; antique cards. www.ehow.com/how_13524_collect-postcards.html

**Posters:** sports, movies, plays.

**Pottery**

**Radios:** tube, transistor, miniature.

**Records (of the phonographic variety):** Some people insist the quality is better than the best digital. Or perhaps you might collect record players.

**Rugs:** by country or culture.

**Scales:** old balance scales for postage, pharmacies, gold.

**Semi-precious Stones**

**Sheet Music:** by genre, period or composer.

**Smoking Paraphernalia**

**Sports-related Items**

**Spurs** www.antiquesjournal.com/Pages04/archives/spurs.html

**Stained Glass:** old churches, home windows.

**Stamps**

**Stock Certificates:** www.antiqueweb.com/articles/stockcollecting.html

**Stoves:** not the kitchen variety, but small camper, WWI or WWII stoves.

**Tea Pots:** novelty, Chinese, Japanese, ceramic, metal.

**Teddie Bears:** you too can be an arctophile (bear lover).

**Telephones:** fiddlebacks, potbellies, coffins — they are all phones.

**Televisions:** wouldn't it be neat to own a Predicta?

**Theater Programs:** historical or ones to which you've been.

**Tokens:** purchase, gaming, transportation, memorial.

**Tools:** antique or by type.

**Toothpick Holders:** think I'm kidding? Here's the link to the National Toothpick Holder Collectors Society. www.nthcs.org

**Toys:** antique or by type.

**Transportation-related Items**

**Trunks:** they can double as furniture and storage bins.

**Typewriters** www.typewritermuseum.org

**Walking Sticks** www.canequest.com

**Wristwatches:** vintage, military, cartoon characters

 Appendix D

## VETERANS' ORGANIZATIONS

**American Ex-Prisoners of War**
3201 East Pioneer Parkway,
#40
Arlington, TX 76010
(817) 649-2979
www.axpow.org

**American G.I. Forum**
2870 N. Speer Blvd.
Suite 220
Denver, CO 80211
(303) 458-1700
(303) 458-1634 Fax
agiforum@uswest.net
www.americangiforum.org

**American Legion**
P.O. Box 1055
Indianapolis, IN 46206
(317) 630-1200
(202) 861-2786 Fax
www.legion.org

**American Veterans Committee**
6309 Bannockburn Drive
Bethesda, MD 20817
(301) 320-6490
(301) 320-6490 Fax
www.americanveteranscenter.org

**American Veterans of WWII,
Korea and Vietnam (AMVETS)**
4647 Forbes Boulevard
Lanham, MD 20706-4380
(301) 459-9600
(301) 459-7924 Fax
amvets@amvets.org
www.amvets.org

**Army and Navy Union,
USA, Inc.**
604 Robbins Ave.
Niles, OH 44446
(330) 307-7049
www.armynavy.net

**Blinded Veterans Association**
477 H Street, NW
Washington, DC   20001-2694
(202) 371-8880
(202) 371-8258 Fax
bva@bva.org
www.bva.org

**Catholic War Veterans,
USA, Inc.**
441 North Lee Street
Alexandria, VA   22314
(703) 549-3622
(703) 684-5196 Fax
www.cwv.org

**Congressional Medal of Honor
Society of the United States of
America**
40 Patriots Point Road
Mt. Pleasant, SC   29464
(843) 884-8862
(843) 884-1471 Fax
www.cmohs.org

**Disabled American Veterans**
3725 Alexandria Pike
Cold Springs, KY   41076
(606) 441-7300
www.dav.org

**Fleet Reserve Association**
125 N. West Street
Alexandria, VA   22314-2754
1 (800) FRA-1924
www.fra.org

**Italian American War Veterans
of the USA**
115 S. Meridian Road
Youngstown, OH   44509
www. itamvets.org

**Jewish War Veterans
of the USA**
1811 R Street, NW
Washington, DC   20009
(202) 265-6280
(202) 234-5662 Fax
jwv@erol.com
www.jvw.org

**Marine Corps League**
8626 Lee Highway
Fairfax, VA 22031
(703) 207-9588
(703) 207-0047 Fax
mcl@mcleague.org
www.mcleague.org

**Military Order of the Purple Heart of the U.S.A., Inc.**
5413-B Backlick Road
Springfield, VA  22151
(703) 642-5360
(703) 642-2054 Fax
info@purpleheart.org

**Military Order of the World Wars**
435 North Lee Street
Alexandria, VA  22314
(703) 683-4911
(703) 683-4501 Fax
www.militaryorder.net

**National Association for Black Veterans, Inc.**
P.O. Box 11432
Milwaukee, WI  53211-0432
1-800-842-4597
(414) 342-0840 Fax
www.nabvets.com

**Non Commissioned Officers Association**
10635 IH 35 North
San Antonio, TX  78233
(703) 549-0311
(703) 549-0245 Fax
www.ncoausa.org

**Paralyzed Veterans of America**
801 18th Street, NW
Washington, DC  20006
(202) 872-1300
(202) 416-7643 Fax
www.pva.org

**Polish Legion of American Veterans, USA**
PO Box 42042
Washington, DC 20015
(727) 848-7826
www.plav.org

**The Retired Enlisted Association**
1111 S. Abilene Court
Aurora, CO 80012-4909
1-800-338-9337
(303) 752-0835 Fax
treahq@trea.org
www.trea.org

**Veterans of Foreign Wars of the United States**
406 West 34th Street
(Broadway at 34th Street)
Kansas City, MO 64111
(816) 756-3390
(202) 543-6719 Fax
www.vfw.org

**Veterans of the Vietnam
War, Inc.**
805 S Township Blvd.
Pittston, PA   18640-3327
1-800-VIETNAM
(570) 603-9740 Fax
www.vnw.org

**Vietnam Veterans
of America, Inc.**
8605 Cameron Street 400
Silver Spring, MD   20910
(301) 585-4000
(301) 585-0519 Fax
www.vva.org

 Appendix E

# VOLUNTEER CONSIDERATIONS AND OPPORTUNITIES

As you think about volunteering, consider issues that are important to you, e.g.:

- Animal Well-Being
- Art and Culture
- Baby Health
- Children
- Civic Issues
- Disabled
- Education
- Elderly
- Employment
- Environment
- Government
- Homelessness
- Human Rights
- Hunger
- Justice
- Literacy
- Refugees
- Religion
- Safety
- Substance Abuse
- Teenagers

Think about the skills you bring to bear while volunteering, e.g.:

- Administration
- Communication
- Computer
- Coordination
- Counseling
- Food Preparation
- Helping Hands
- Organization
- Planning
- Professional
- Reading

- Social
- Teaching
- Trades
- Transportation

Think about the amount of time that you wish to contribute:

- A few hours every week?
- A few hours every day?
- Full-time?

Would you prefer activities that are regularly scheduled and fairly consistent or would you prefer to be in more of a project-oriented environment?

You can learn about volunteering opportunities from a variety of sources, e.g.:

- American Association of Retired People — www.aarp.org
- American Red Cross — www.redcross.org
- AmeriCorps — www.americorps.gov
- Arts Councils
- Chambers of Commerce
- Churches
- Civic Ventures — www.civicventures.org
- Corporation for National and Community Service — www.nationalservice.org
- Easter Seals Society — www.easterseals.com
- Executive Service Corps (links retired execs with nonprofits and public-service agencies) — www.escus.org

- Experience Corps (focuses on literacy) – www.experiencecorps.org
- Foster Grandparents – www.fostergrandparentprogram.org
- Goodwill Industries – www.goodwill.org
- Habitat for Humanity – www.habitat.org
- Humane Society of the United States – www.hsus.org
- Literacy Volunteers of America – www.literacyvlounteers.org
- Local government
- March of Dimes – www.modimes.org
- Mentor (links mentors with schools and civic organizations) – www.mentor.org
- Mosques
- National Retiree Volunteer Coalition (helps retirees volunteer with former employers on various educational, environmental and community issues) www.nrvc.org
- Nature Conservancy – www.nature.org
- Peace Corps (international service volunteering) – www.peacecorps.gov
- Plan Canada (formerly Foster Parents Plan) – www.plancanada.ca
- Planned Parenthood – www.plannedparenthood.org
- RSVP (Retired and Senior Volunteer Program) – www.seniorcorps.ogov/about/programs/rsvp.asp
- Salvation Army – www.salvationarmy.org
- Save the Children – www.savethechildren.org

- Senior Companions — www.seniorcorps.gov/about/programs/sc.asp
- Senior Corps — www.seniorcorps.org
- Synagogues
- United Way — www.national.unitedway.org
- USA Freedom Corps — www.usafreedomcorps.gov
- VolunteerMatch — www.volunteermatch.org
- Volunteers in Medicine (links retired medical professional to people in need) — www.volunteersinmedicine.org
- Volunteers of America — www.voa.org

# ABOUT THE AUTHOR

## Living What I Preach

So, I've written a book on the importance of staying intellectually, socially and physically engaged in retirement. I've even been bold enough to title it: *The Successful Retirement Guide*. It becomes reasonable to ask:

Am I living what I preach?

Since "retiring" from life in a big corporation, I have written a set of goals for each year. I divide them into categories of intellectual, social and physical with usually six to ten goals in each category. I monitor my progress throughout the year; add, delete or modify goals as conditions change; and I give each goal a rating of "accomplished" or "not accomplished" at year-end. Goals that were not accomplished may be carried over into the following year. (Full disclosure: Part of my career was in Human Resources.)

So, what's been accomplished, and what am I doing?

One major accomplishment has been this book. It took longer than I anticipated to write, longer than I anticipated to link up with a publisher, and longer than I anticipated to get it into your hands. But here it is!

Another accomplishment has been travel. While I was working, most travel was for business or vacation (aka: time away from work, usually with offspring, usually for a week at a time and not too far away). Now travel is usually for more than a week, frequently farther away and, most importantly, I have much more time for learning in advance about the geography, history, art, architecture, food, beverages, languages, religions, governments and social customs of the places my wife Barbara and I will visit. I try to drive my own car when traveling to keep the itinerary flexible, and I like to incorporate lots of walking — for the exercise certainly, but also to get an enhanced feeling for the cities and countryside.

Where have I been since retiring five years ago? I have been fortunate to have had the opportunity to hike Italy's Cinque Terra, scale Brunelleschi's dome in Florence, cruise the canals in Venice, explore the forums of ancient Rome, attend the opera in Vicenza, sample cheese and truffles (the fungal variety) in Bologna, sniff the sulfurous fumes of Volcano in the Aeolian Islands, climb Mount Aetna, follow the whiskey trail in Scotland (like Napa, but with more fire in the belly), sing in a pub in Kenmare, camp and ride a camel in the Sahara, explore the Medina in Marrakech, float down the Ganges River at sunrise, ride an elephant into a Raja's fort, photocapture a leopard in Kenya, tour the windmills in Holland's Kinderdijk, sample chocolate in Belgium and sail in Belize, the Bahamas, the Carribean and up the east coast of the U.S.

Travel and sailing (particularly if you can bareboat (meaning you are the captain, not that you are naked)) are great activities because they can nicely encompass the intellectual, social and physical. But travel is limited for most of us by constraints of money and other responsibilities. So, while I look forward to more travel and sailing, what am I up to on a more day-to-day basis?

## For my mind . . .

I study Italian — in classes and on my own. While language study is good intellectually, some knowledge of Italian can also be helpful in restaurants and makes travel in Italy (one of my favorite places to visit) much more enjoyable.

I study music theory using a keyboard and guitar. And I work at improving my proficiency as a guitar player using my Gibson J-45 acoustic and Les Paul electric.

I read at least one intellectually stimulating, non-fiction book a month. I place no limits on my fiction reading.

I participate in several courses or learning programs each year. The subject matter is quite diverse. One course of particular interest to me was Calculus. It was the only course in which I had done poorly during my academic years. I promised myself that someday I would revisit it and really understand it. Mission accomplished.

I play at becoming a better bridge and chess player. I do crossword and soduku puzzles every day.

## For my body . . .

Yoga and stretching: My wife convinced me to join her yoga class (I was usually the only guy), and I came away thoroughly convinced of its value for strength, flexibility and balance. I do 30-40 minutes of stretching and yoga every morning.

Walking: I do four miles a day outdoors in reasonable weather; in less attractive conditions I use a treadmill. In the summer I add swimming half a mile several times a week. In the winter, I add snowshoeing, if the weatherman has been kind enough to provide some snow.

Weights: I use free and machine weights every other day.

Weight: I also have a weight (reduction) goal. I have had this goal for five years. I am sure I will achieve it...one of these years.

## For socialization . . .

Prior to retirement, my social activities were largely tied to my 9-to-10 hours a day at work and a small circle of friends and relatives. Post retirement, I still have the circle of friends and relatives, and on occasion see folks from where I used to work, but with the loss of 50 hours of interaction from the workplace, there is a need for me to make sure my other activities incorporate a social aspect, e.g. walk *with* someone; walk with my golden retriever puppy Rufus, "the chick magnet" (he introduces me to all sorts of people); take classes that involve class interaction; choose volunteer activities that involve working with others; travel with other couples.

Becoming an author is also good for socialization. While the initial drafting may be mostly a solo activity, the promotion and selling of a book requires a lot of interaction.

And I have been able to explore personally many of the activities discussed in this book – this was certainly part of the fun of researching it – and I am looking forward to further discoveries of interesting things to do.

Finally, I am working to declutter my life. It seems like we go through life accumulating all sorts of stuff – books, clothes, records, tools, photos, furniture, luggage, decorative items, bicycles, hardware, software, games, sports equipment, old socks and so on. While there are some things I want to retain for practical or sentimental reasons, there is a bunch of stuff that I don't need and wouldn't miss and which can thus be sold, donated or trashed. I am not completely sure why, but decluttering leaves me with a sense of increased freedom and mental space (in addition to the physical space the "clutter" formerly occupied).

Overall, I see myself as a work in progress. I want to explore as many roads as I can along the way. My life is worth living, and I'm having great fun living it!